Clothes
without
patterns

Fay Morgan

Photographs by Deenie Yudell

Mills & Boon Limited
London Toronto Sydney

First published in Great Britain 1977 by Mills & Boon
Limited, 17–19 Foley Street, London W1A 1DR.

© Fay Morgan 1977

Reprinted 1980

ISBN 0 263 06449 2

Printed in Great Britain by
M. & A. Thomson Litho Limited, East Kilbride
and bound by Hunter & Foulis, Edinburgh.

Contents

Introduction

We are more free in our way of dress today than we have ever been. Throughout history, styles of dress have been dictated by class or work systems and as a method of attraction to the opposite sex. Clothes that are now becoming more dominant are those that are practical for our work and leisure activities.

We can change our clothes and their styles everyday, and we are pressured into this change by the commercial aspects of our world. The commercial market offers many styles of dress, but we are limited in our choice by the fashion makers. Most clothes are mass-produced, budgeting the costs to make the items as saleable as possible. Where clothes are individually designed, then one pays for a unique or personal style.

To opt out of the system of mass-produced, ready-made clothes, we can make our own garments to suit our individual needs. There is no revelation in making one's own clothes. One can buy a pattern, fabric and all the trimmings, snip and stitch away for hours and end up with a hand-made garment, yet mass-produced in style.

Can we not think for ourselves? Do we need complex clothes? What are our individual needs for clothing our bodies? Why do we need clothes at all?

This last question may seem childish, but it returns our thoughts to our basic needs. The logical answer is that we wear clothes to protect ourselves from extremes of temperature, but what if we live in a climate where we would be most comfortable without clothing? Is clothing then used for the sake of morality? This question gives rise to a mass of psychological interpretations. Another answer could be for ornamentation, to attract, or to please oneself, or to cover up faults.

Body adornment could be interpreted as decorating the body by the use of paint or dye, by covering it with a skin, a desirable piece of cloth or other material.

How shall we cover our bodies? Basically, our bodies are structures on which we can hang, wrap or tie, or fasten by other methods, our clothing or coverings. For many centuries, the basic body covering was a length of cloth wrapped and tied round the body. This developed into simple clothing structures, such as tunics, with or without sleeves. At times a single garment was worn; at others, many layers of clothing. These changes did not always depend on the climatic conditions, but on fashion systems. A study of the history of fashion points out the development and oddity of fashion styles.

Some garments still being worn today are of a similar style to those wrapped and tied garments of the first civilizations. These garments are usually associated with peasant cultures, until an analogy is made with ecclesiastical garments, which have not changed since medieval times. They are worn not because the culture has remained static, but because the garments are suited to their function. They protect the body from cold and heat, are comfortable to wear and attractive to look at. Most important, they are easy to make, using the fabric economically.

The system of designing the garments in this book makes use of basic shapes: squares, rectangles, circles and triangles. The instructions presuppose some background in sewing techniques, or that you will know where to get supplementary information should you need to. However, as some of the garments are exceptionally easy to make from one or two squares, or rectangles, beginners to dressmaking might find these a good starting point. The making up of each garment is explained stage by stage and the basic hand-sewing techniques originally used for all the garments are described at the end of the book.

From these simple shapes, complex structures of multiple basic shapes can be developed. All the garments can be adapted to suit your needs. You could start off with one garment and find yourself with a whole wardrobe based on these simple shapes. Unique garments can be the result of working out your own combinations of shapes.

Because of the use of basic shapes, no paper patterns are

needed. The layouts for the shapes differ from commercial paper patterns in that it is not necessary to have spaces between the pieces, so you are not wasting fabric. You may waste some fabric if patterned material is used that needs to be matched up, but this also occurs in ordinary paper pattern dressmaking.

The sizing of the layouts is based on an average adult female, 1·7 m (5′ 6″) tall, with a 92 cm (36″) bust, except where otherwise stated. Hem and seam allowances are contained within the layouts and are normally 2·5 cm (1″).

To ensure that the layout of the garment is your size, carefully take your own measurements at the relevant parts, add hem and seam allowances to all sides of the basic unit shape and allow a bit extra for ease of movement within the garment. If you need to change the given layout for larger or smaller sizes, or for wider widths of fabric, make a scaled-down chart on graph paper, 10 cm equal to 1 m (1″ equal to 1′). Change the layout to your required size and rearrange pieces if necessary. This may be daunting, but as many of the garments are loose fitting, they can be worn equally successfully by many adult sizes without having to radically alter the sizes given.

Fabric is available in a variety of widths and is now being sold by the metre, and fractions of a metre, in Great Britain. The traditional widths of 24″, 36″, 48″, 54″ and 60″ are still being used, but are now mostly expressed in whole centimetres: 61 cm, 90 cm, 120 cm, 140 cm and 150 cm respectively. These conversions are, of course, only equivalents and are not accurate. Therefore, they are only used on the layouts in this book for the *width* of the fabric shown. Elsewhere, more accurate conversions from inches and feet to centimetres and metres are used. This discrepancy will continue until fabric widths are actually woven to metric sizes.

Different fabric widths are used for most of the layouts in this book, depending on the most economical way of cutting the cloth. Where wastage does occur, this can always be used to make a belt or trim for the garment.

The information given on page 8 is a simple key to the layouts and working diagrams used throughout the book.

This has been used, where needed, to show the right side of the fabric.

Wastage

Cutting line ————
Fold line — — —

In some of the layouts, the fabric is folded so that the pattern pieces are cut double. The fabric in a layout is usually folded lengthwise. At other stages of making up a garment, the fabric is folded lengthwise or crosswise. See page 150 for a detailed explanation of these terms.

The use of interesting fabrics when making a garment greatly enhances its distinctive quality. Because of the economical layouts, the amount of fabric required is usually less than that required in conventional patterns. Therefore, a better quality of fabric can be purchased. Often the most exciting fabrics are found in the furnishings section of a store and not in the dress fabrics department. Some garments could be made up from crocheted, or hand-knitted, pieces, or a special fabric could be hand-woven.

Throughout the book, craft techniques, such as embroidery, have been mentioned to use in combination with, or to embellish, the clothes. These techniques have not been explained in detail, but a list of books for further reading is given on page 159.

Some of the garments can only be made up from fabrics that are plain, have an all-over texture, or a two-way pattern. In these cases one-way patterns or napped fabrics cannot be used. A one-way pattern is one that can only be seen the correct way up from one crossway view of the fabric (see page 150). A napped fabric, such as velvet, corduroy or fur, is a fabric or skin constructed with a sloping pile. These fabrics feel rough when stroked against the pile (nap) and smooth when stroked in the opposite direction. They also appear darker or lighter when looked at with, or against, the pile (nap). Napped fabrics should be cut so that all pieces stroke smoothly in the same direction, usually top to bottom of garment.

Linings have not been mentioned except in the form of backing pieces for strengthening shoulders, etc. This is because the type of clothes, or the simple constructions, do not need linings. However, if you wish to line any of the garments, you will need the same amount of lining fabric as the requirements given for the garment, or portion of the garment.

Seams are normally stitched by placing the right sides of the fabric together; the exception is for a french seam. All seams should be neatened after stitching. Try on the garment during successive stages of making up to ensure a good fit.

Pressing the fabric at each stage of making up the garment is most important. Always press the section of the garment you have been working on before stitching it to another section. Good pressing gives any garment a professional finish.

There is never just one way of doing anything and there are many ways of making up these garments. Simple techniques are used in making up the garments in this book and though some of these are unconventional, they do work. I hope that you will enjoy making up and wearing these garments, and that you will feel encouraged to design and embellish many more.

Serape

This garment is a type of poncho that has its origins in South America. It is constructed from two rectangular pieces of fabric and is extremely easy to cut out and make up.

Fabric requirements

For a child or small adult: the two rectangles are cut from 0·9 m (1 yd) of 90 cm (36″) fabric.

For an average adult: the two rectangles should each measure 61 cm × 122 cm (24″ × 48″), so 1·2 m (1⅓ yds) of 120 cm (48″) fabric, or 2·4 m (2⅔ yds) of 61 cm (24″) fabric are required.

For a large adult: 1·8 m (2 yds) of 140 cm (54″) fabric, or 3·7 m (4 yds) of 90 cm (36″) fabric.

As this garment is intended as a cover-up for warmth, suitable fabrics to choose are all types of wools, worsteds and blends. Woven, knitted or crocheted materials can also be used. Stripes look very effective made up into a serape, but one-way designs and napped fabrics should be avoided.

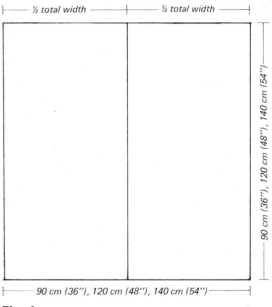

Fig. 1

Making up

Lay out fabric as shown in Figs 1 or 2, and cut in half at centre, or knit/crochet two rectangles to the required size.

If woven or knitted jersey fabrics are used, hem or bind all edges of both rectangles.

With right sides together, place the short edge of one rectangle to half of the long side of the second rectangle and oversew the edges together (Fig. 3). Take the unattached short edge of the second rectangle, place it against the unattached half of the long side of the first rectangle and oversew the edges together (Fig. 4).

If using a stretchy fabric it is advisable to bind or face the neck opening with straight tape to prevent the neck from stretching out of shape.

The lower edges of the serape can be fringed to provide some decoration. Cut lengths of yarn measuring just over twice the required length of the fringe. Make a small hole about 1 cm ($\frac{1}{2}$″) from the edge by inserting a crochet hook. Centre the strands over the hook and pull them through the hole to form a loop. Work the ends of yarn through this loop and pull to tighten the knot (Fig. 5).

Fig. 2

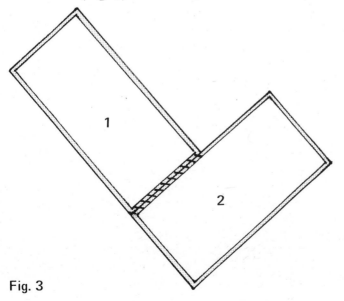

Fig. 3

13

Alternatively, you could stitch a ready-made fringe or trim to all the outer edges of the serape.

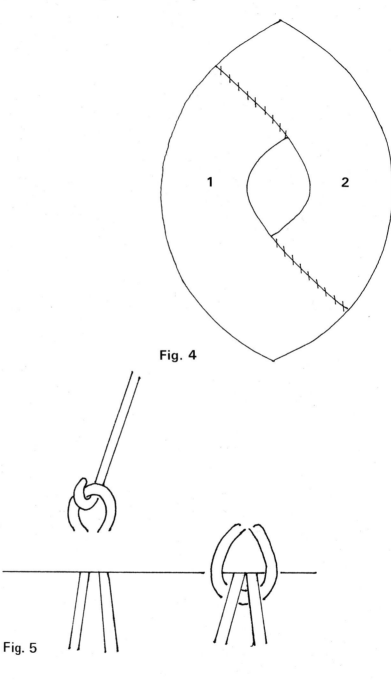

Fig. 4

Fig. 5

Ruana

A ruana is another type of poncho from South America. It can be made from a single rectangle of fabric, or two rectangles to form one large rectangle.

Fabric requirements

For a child: depending on the length required, 1·2 m–1·5 m (1⅓ yds–1⅔ yds) of 90 cm (36″) fabric.
For an adult: 1·8 m (2 yds) of 120 cm (48″) fabric, or at least 1·8 m (2 yds) of 140 cm (54″) fabric. If using two rectangles to form one large rectangle, 3·7 m (4 yds) of 61 cm (24″) fabric.

Suitable fabrics are all types of wools, worsteds and blends, but avoid using fabrics with a one-way design or nap.

Making up

Single-piece ruana: lay out fabric as shown in Fig. 1 and cut down the centre to 15 cm (6″) beyond centre point. Neaten these cut edges by hemming or blanket stitch (Fig. 3). The lower edges may be hemmed, embroidered or fringed, as for the serape. A decorative finish may also be taken down both sides of the ruana.

Double-piece ruana: for a 61 cm (24″) fabric, cut fabric in half to form two pieces each measuring 1·8 m (2 yds) by 61 cm (24″). Place the two halves lengthways together and stitch to within 15 cm (6″) of the centre point to form back seam (Fig. 2). Finish the edges as for one-piece ruana.

The ruana is worn with the opening at the front of the body—loose, belted, or with one of the front pieces flipped over the opposite shoulder.

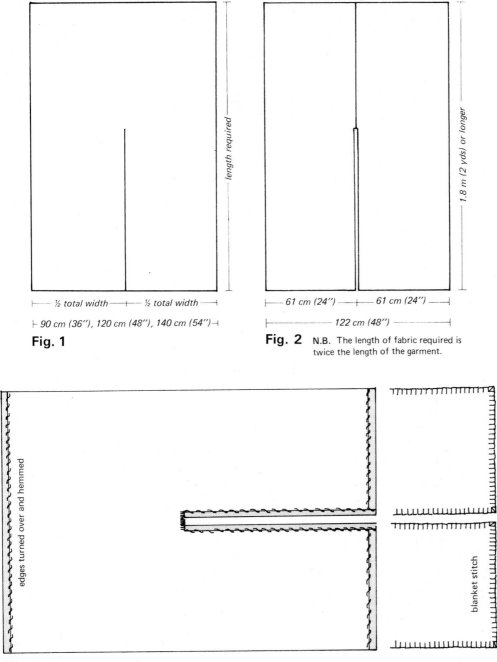

½ total width ——— ½ total width

90 cm (36"), 120 cm (48"), 140 cm (54")

Fig. 1

61 cm (24") ——— 61 cm (24")

122 cm (48")

Fig. 2 N.B. The length of fabric required is twice the length of the garment.

length required

1.8 m (2 yds) or longer

edges turned over and hemmed

blanket stitch

Fig. 3

Poncho developments

ONE-PIECE PONCHO

A variation of the ruana is the one-piece poncho, either a square or a rectangle, with a small slit for the neck opening.

Fabric requirements

For a child or small adult: a square poncho requires 0·9 m (1 yd) of 90 cm (36″) fabric. A rectangular poncho requires up to 1·8 m (2 yds) of 90 cm (36″) fabric.

For an adult: a square poncho requires 1·2 m (1⅓ yds) of 120 cm (48″) fabric. A rectangular poncho requires up to 2·4 m (2⅔ yds) of 120 cm (48″) fabric.

For a large adult: a square poncho requires 1·4 m (1½ yds) of 140 cm (54″) fabric. A rectangular poncho requires up to 2·7 m (3 yds) of 140 cm (54″) fabric.

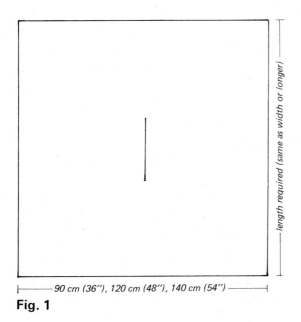

length required (same as width or longer)

|—— 90 cm (36″), 120 cm (48″), 140 cm (54″) ——|

Fig. 1

As these ponchos are of such simple construction, a lot can be achieved by the use of interesting fabrics. A double cloth (reversible) fabric is traditionally used for the ruana to show either side of the material. The other ponchos would look equally effective made up in double, or reversible, fabrics so that they can be worn either side out.

Making up

The making up of this garment is similar to the ruana. Lay out fabric as shown in Fig. 1. Cut a slit through the centre point, approximately 31 cm–36 cm (12"–14") in length, so that the poncho can be pulled over the head. Neaten this slit with binding or stitching.

If the fabric you have chosen is not wide enough at 90 cm (36"), add a decorative border or edging of, say, 15 cm (6") all round the poncho, thus bringing the size up to a 120 cm (48") width.

The poncho can be worn with its lower edges parallel to the ground. (**Note**: When the arms are dropped the lower edges fall in a curve with the outer points nearer the ground.) Or the poncho can be set at an angle so that the four corners are pointing towards the ground.

FOUR-PIECE PONCHO

A development variation of the one-piece poncho is a construction of four pieces: two large rectangles and two long inset rectangles. See the colour photograph facing page 49.

Fabric requirements

For small adults: if using the same fabric throughout, 120 cm (48″) wide × twice the desired length, i.e. measure from shoulder to calf and double this measurement for back and front of garment—approximately 1·8 m (2 yds).

For an average or large adult: if using the same fabric throughout, 2·7 m (3 yds) of 140 cm (54″) fabric (using the same length calculations as above). 90 cm (36″) fabric can be used with the alternative layout shown in Fig. 2, in which case 5·5 m (6 yds) are required.

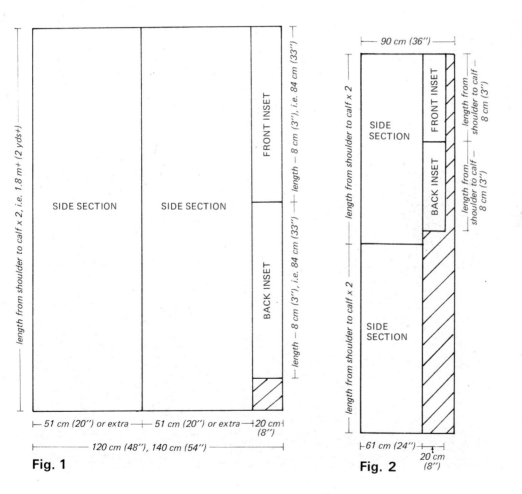

Fig. 1

Fig. 2

Woollens and other warm fabrics are especially suitable. Corduroy, brocades and quilted cottons can also be used. Knitted fabrics, unless bonded, are not suitable as they have a tendency to sag and pull out of shape when used in large pieces. Fabrics with a one-way design or nap can be used, but cut the side sections in two on the shoulder line and turn sections so that the fabric hangs the correct way up on back and front of garment. Add an extra 5 cm (2″) to length requirements for these extra shoulder seams.

The garment can be made more interesting by using different fabrics for the inset and main sections; plain fabric for the large rectangles and patterned fabric for the insets, or vice versa. The insets can be embroidered in many ways to contrast with plain rectangles.

Making up

Lay out fabric as shown in Figs 1 or 2 and cut out the four pieces. If any embroidery or other embellishment is going to be worked on the inset pieces, complete this before stitching the sections together.

Pin the two inset pieces between the two large rectangles, leaving an opening for the neck. Hem or bind the raw edges of the neck opening and stitch the insets in place. Finish off the rest of the raw edges by fringing, at the bottom of the poncho, or by stitching (Fig. 3).

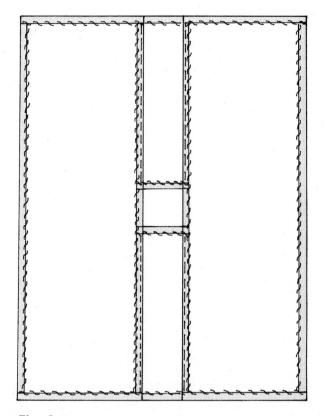

Fig. 3 Pieces in position, stitched together and edges neatened.

Cover-up garments
based on rectangles

An infinite variety of garments may be constructed from the rectangle and the square. The more basic ponchos can become full jackets and long coat-type ponchos. Tunics and dresses can also be developed from these simple shapes. Three possibilities in construction and cut are explored in this section:

  horizontal line—three- and four-piece garments
  vertical line—three- and four-piece garments
  combination of horizontal and vertical with an inset at centre back and front—six-piece garments.

HORIZONTAL

These are garments in which the major line is horizontal. They range from a short jacket to a long cover-up. See the colour photograph facing page 64.

Fabric requirements

The requirements vary according to the width of fabric available and the desired length of garment. However, approximate requirements are as follows.

For long sleeves: allow 61 cm (24″) for depth of sleeve × measurement of arms extended (i.e. from wrist of one hand, across back, to wrist of other hand), plus two seam allowances.
For each body piece: the measurement from the under arm to length desired, plus two seam allowances.

For 90 cm (36″) fabric the layout is in one long strip (Fig. 1). For plain, textured or all-over patterned fabrics in 120 cm–150 cm (48″–60″) widths, the body pieces can be cut sideways, either as rectangles or as trapeziums (Fig. 2). (A trapezium is a quadrilateral that has two of its sides parallel.) Tapering a rectangle to a trapezium gives the garment a more flowing line.

On the widest widths, 140 cm–150 cm (54″–60″), fabrics with a one-way design or nap can be used (Fig. 3), but cut the top piece in two along the shoulder line and turn one piece so that the fabric is the correct way up on back and front of garment. This also applies to narrow-width fabrics (Fig. 1).

All types and weights of fabrics are suitable. However, caution must be used in the choice of pattern for the layout in Fig. 2, as any motif on the fabric will be cut sideways on.

Making up

Lay out fabric as shown in Figs 1, 2 or 3. If using fabric with a one-way design or nap, cut top piece in two on shoulder line. Cut out pieces.

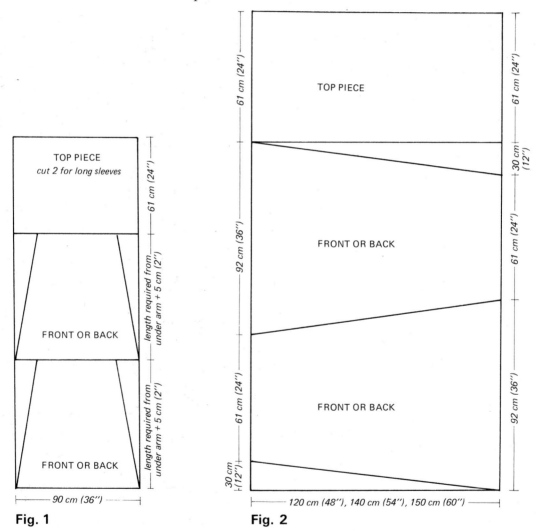

Fig. 1   **Fig. 2**

If planning long sleeves and using 90 cm (36″) fabric, cut two top pieces, place them side by side and join at centre back. Leave centre front seam open to allow for easy head entry. On wider fabrics the top section, including the sleeves, is cut in one piece.

The neckline should be cut a little to the front of the centre point of the shoulder line, about 2·5 cm (1″) forward. This is because one's neck is set forward on one's shoulders and the neck opening will fit neatly round the neck if cut in this way (Fig. 4).

To calculate the neck measurements of a close-fitting circular neckline (Fig. 6), take a tape measure, or a piece of string, and measure the circumference at the base of the neck. The next stage can be worked out in two ways.

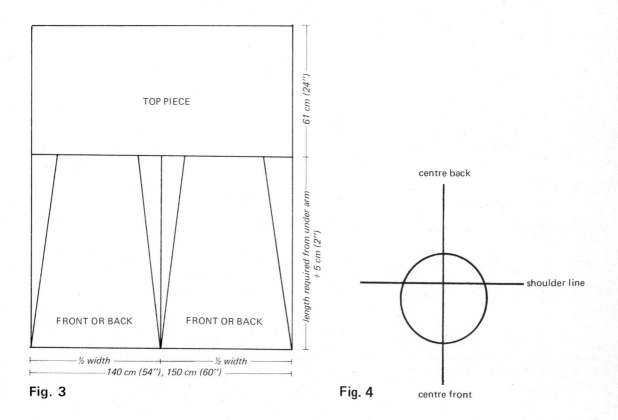

Fig. 3

Fig. 4

1 The mathematical formula for calculating the diameter of a circle with a known circumference is:

$$\frac{\text{circumference}}{\pi \text{ (pi)}} = \text{diameter} \quad (\pi = \frac{22}{7} \text{ or } 3\cdot1416)$$

Therefore, if the circumference of the neckline is 36 cm, the calculation is worked out as follows:

$$\frac{36 \times 7}{22} \text{ cancels down to } \frac{18 \times 7}{11} = \frac{126}{11} = 11\cdot4 \text{ cm (diameter)}.$$

As the radius is half the diameter, your final working measurement is 5·7 cm.

The same calculation worked out in inches (circumference = 14″):

$$\frac{14 \times 7}{22} \text{ cancels down to } \frac{7 \times 7}{11} = \frac{49}{11} = 4\tfrac{1}{2}″ \text{ (diameter)}.$$

Therefore, the radius is $2\tfrac{1}{4}″$.

Alternatively, the diameter can be calculated by dividing the decimal calculation of π (3·1416) into the circumference.

2 Form the tape measure or string into a circle and measure across the diameter with a ruler, then divide this measurement in half to obtain the radius.

When planning the neckline of a garment, remember that the measurement you have taken will become the stitching line and the cutting line, or circle, will be smaller than your measured circle. For example, if your neck measures 36 cm (14″), the diameter measured will be 11 cm (4½″). Therefore, you should cut the neckline to a diameter of 10 cm (4″) to give a 1 cm (½″) seam allowance.

To draw the circle on your fabric, take a length of thread and stabilize one end by pinning it to the centre point of the intended circle. With a marker (pointed chalk) fixed on the thread at the radius length, draw a circle for the cutting line. Then move marker and draw a circle for the stitching line.

For a looser neckline a larger circle may be cut. If the neckline has no other opening to allow head entry, the circumference

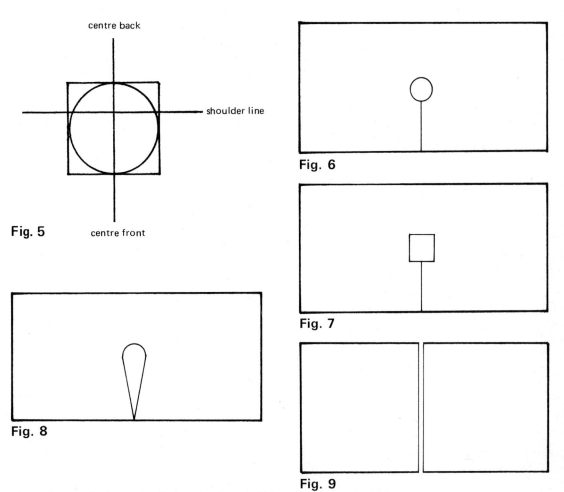

Fig. 5

centre back

shoulder line

centre front

Fig. 6

Fig. 7

Fig. 8

Fig. 9

should be taken around the head and hair, so that when the garment is made up, the neckline will easily slip over the head.

To calculate a square neckline (Fig. 7), measure as for round neck and draw a circle on a piece of paper. Draw a square on the outer side of the circle, so that the circle touches the square at the centre points of its four sides (Fig. 5). Cut out square and place on fabric, with the centre points together. Move square 2·5 cm (1″) forward. Draw round square on to the fabric for stitching line, then draw another square, 1 cm ($\frac{1}{2}$″) in from stitching line for a cutting line.

For a looser square neckline, the same measuring and marking processes apply as described above.

31

Horizontal-line
cover-up showing
one-piece hood

A V-neckline (Fig. 8) may be made by using the same calculations as for a circular neckline. Mark out half of the circle for the back of the neck, then draw straight lines from both sides of the semicircle to the centre front of the garment. The longer the lines to the centre point, the deeper the V-neckline will be. With this type of neckline on horizontal-line garments, the V needs to be long enough for the head to easily enter the garment.

A slit neckline can be cut on horizontal-line garments by cutting the top piece in two (Fig. 9), or by cutting a slit through the front half of the top piece to a point approximately 13 cm (5″) beyond the centre point. This gives the neckline a closed back and open front to the top piece. With slit necklines, the fabric does not lie flat, but curves up and round the neck, and the fabric on the shoulders and arms will drop slightly as the neck pushes open the slit.

Neaten neckline and front opening using bias binding or facing (Fig. 10). Cut notches for ease in the seam allowance of neckline (Fig. 10). The binding, or facing, can be completely turned to the inside and hemmed, or can be left visible as a trim on the right side of the garment. (See pages 153–7.)

Centre the top and body pieces at back and front and stitch (Fig. 11). Note that the garment is still in a flat form at this stage.

Fold garment in half and stitch underarm and side seams (Fig. 12).

Because of the simplicity of the cut of these garments, the bottoms of sleeves and hems do not always hang as evenly as with tailored patterns. With some garments, such as the ponchos, this does not matter, but with jackets and dresses, this uneven hang of the garment is not pleasing to our accustomed way of thinking of straight hemlines. You will find that the garment drops at the sides and the sleeves if you are standing with your arms down at your sides. If you raise your arms to a horizontal position, the dropped areas become level. However, most of the time one's hands are below the horizontal line of the shoulders and, therefore, the line of the garment is not level.

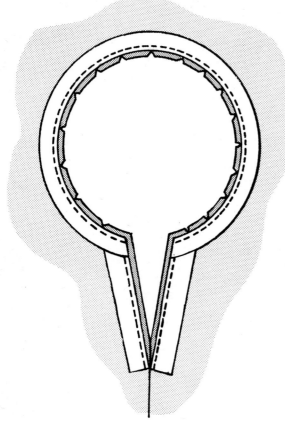
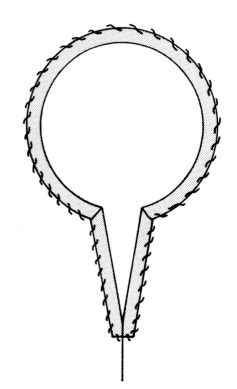

Fig. 10

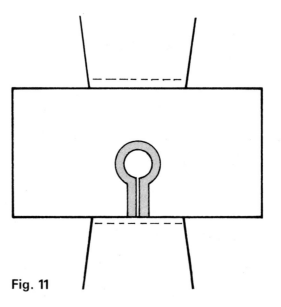

Fig. 11

34

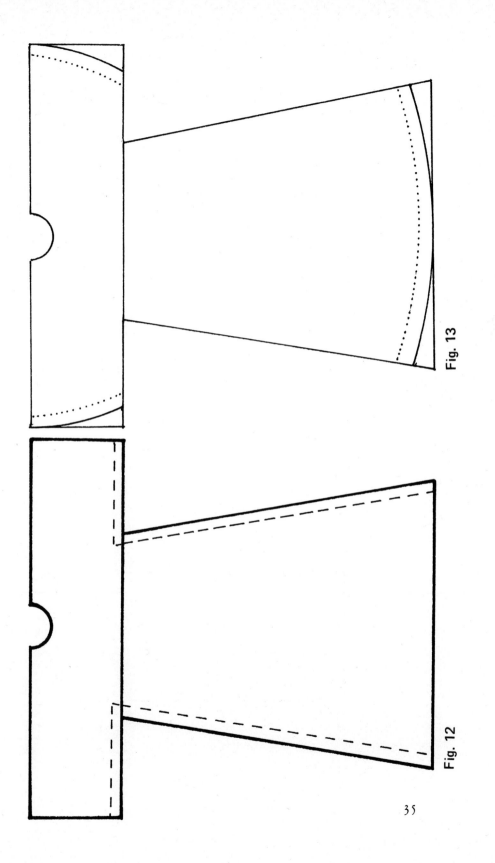

Fig. 13

Fig. 12

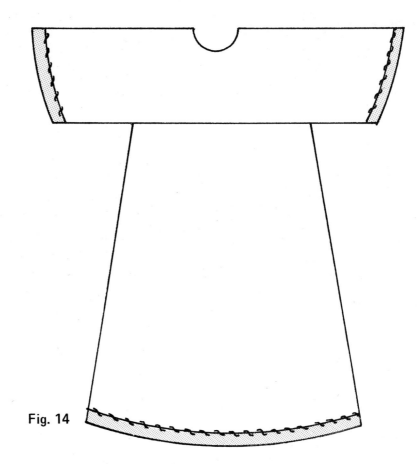

Fig. 14

To rectify this the dropped section is cut off in the form of an arc, so that the length of the garment hangs evenly. Try on the garment and mark the level required on the sleeves and lower edge. Add an allowance for a hem of 5 cm (2″) and cut fabric (Fig. 13).

Finish sleeves and lower edge by hemming or bias binding (Fig. 14).

VERTICAL

These are garments in which the major line is vertical. They range from a short jacket to a long cover-up. If the sleeves are omitted, the result is a tabard.

Fabric requirements

As for the horizontal garments, approximate requirements only are given.

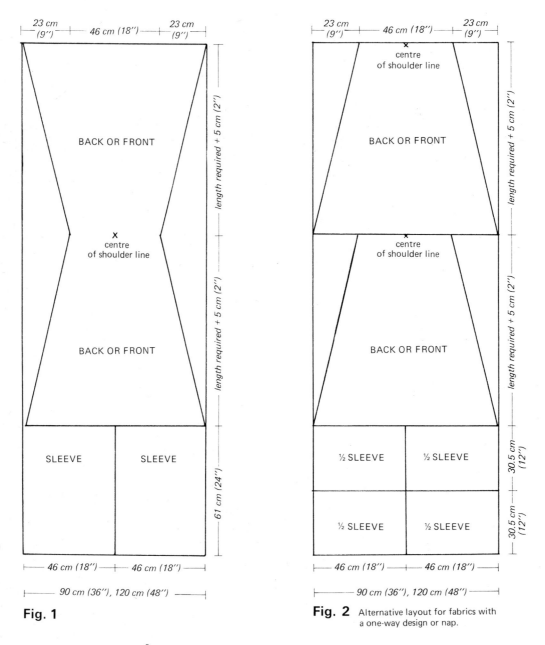

Fig. 1

Fig. 2 Alternative layout for fabrics with a one-way design or nap.

38

If using 90 cm (36″) or 120 cm (48″) fabric, you will need twice the desired length (for back and front of garment) plus 61 cm (24″) for both sleeves plus 15 cm (6″) for seams.

The body of the garment can be cut out as a rectangle, or tapered to the shoulder line in a double trapezium for a more flowing line. If the rectangular form is kept, less length of sleeve is required because the sleeves join the body piece further down the arm.

Suitable fabrics include all types and weights of fabrics. However, knitted fabrics, unless bonded, are not suitable, as the length of the body piece may make the fabric sag. Fabrics with a one-way design or nap can be used with the layout shown in Fig. 2.

Making up

Lay out fabric as shown in Figs 1 or 2 and cut out the pieces.

If using a fabric with a one-way design or nap, stitch the shoulder and 'overarm' sleeve seams.

Finish neck opening as for the horizontal garments.

Match the centre points of tops of sleeves and body piece and stitch sleeves to body piece (Fig. 3). The garment is still in a flat form at this stage.

Stitch underarm and side seams of body piece. The side seams can be left partly open and neatened for open-sided tunics, which can be worn with trousers or skirts (Fig. 4).

Try on garment and arc off sleeves and lower edge if necessary (Fig. 5 and see pages 33–5). Hem or bind sleeves and lower edge.

A tie belt or sash can look attractive. A matching or contrasting fabric can be used, or, perhaps, a completely different technique, such as braiding or macramé. Make the belt long enough to allow the ties to hang down gracefully, so emphasizing the vertical line of the garment.

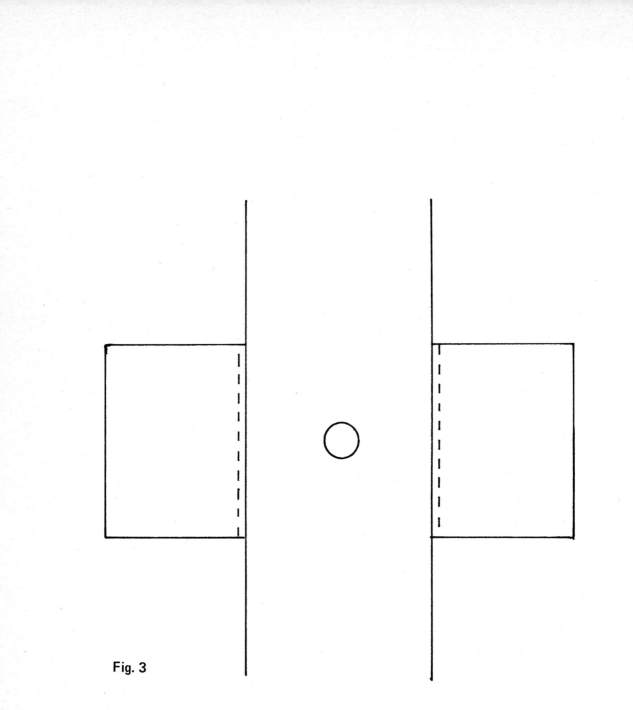

Fig. 3

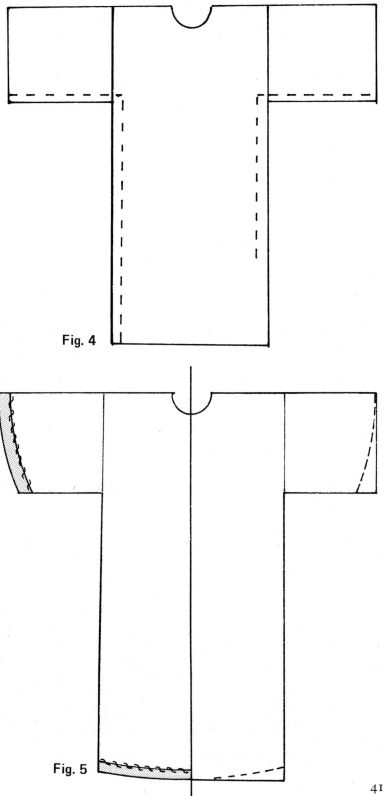

Fig. 4

Fig. 5

COMBINATION

These garments are of a similar style to the horizontal and vertical garments, but employ both features by means of an inset at the back and front.

Fabric requirements

For a child or small adult: a short tunic requires 1·2 m (1⅓ yds) of 90 cm (36″) fabric.

For an average adult: a short tunic requires 1·4 m (1½ yds) of 120 cm (48″) fabric. A long, straight tunic, using the same layout as shown in Fig. 1, requires 2 m (2¼ yds) of 120 cm (48″) or 140 cm (54″) fabric.

If using a narrow width fabric, the extra length can be calculated by allowing 61 cm (24″) × 2 for sleeves, which is inclusive of seams, plus twice the desired length of garment, plus 8 cm (3″) for seams. The length of the garment will be the length you need minus 28 cm (11″), which is the finished depth of sleeve. Add 15 cm (6″) for the insets.

The fabric required for the layout shown in Fig. 2 is calculated in the same way as for narrow-width fabrics.

If using a plain fabric, or one with a two-way design, 2·4 m (2⅔ yds) of 120 cm (48″) or 140 cm (54″) fabric are required (Fig. 3).

Most fabrics are suitable, but avoid using those with a one-way design or nap. If cutting the body section of tunic sideways on, only use all-over patterned or plain fabrics.

Making up

Lay out fabric as shown in Figs 1, 2 or 3 and cut out the pieces.

If using a thick fabric, only cut two insets in the fabric and cut the other two insets in a lining fabric.

On plain fabric it can be attractive to embellish the insets with embroidery, appliqué or quilting. This should be worked before the garment is made up.

Stitch the double thickness inset squares to sleeves. Hem or bind the neck opening (Fig. 4).

Centre body pieces to top section and stitch (Fig. 5). The garment is still in a flat form at this stage.

Fold garment in half and stitch underarm and side seams (Fig. 6). The side seams may be left partly open for a slit-sided tunic.

Arc off sleeves and lower edge if necessary (see page 35). Hem or bind sleeves and lower edge.

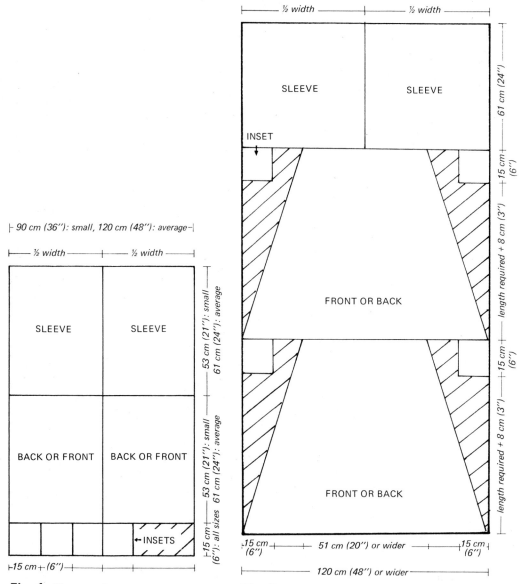

Fig. 2

Fig. 1 Short tunic

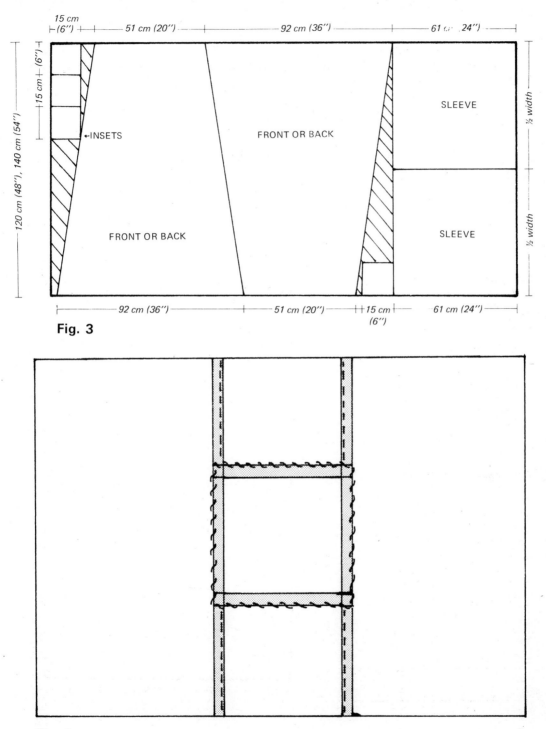

15 cm (6")
15 cm (6")
51 cm (20")
92 cm (36")
61 cm (24")

120 cm (48"), 140 cm (54")

INSETS
FRONT OR BACK
SLEEVE
½ width

FRONT OR BACK
SLEEVE
½ width

92 cm (36")
51 cm (20")
15 cm (6")
61 cm (24")

Fig. 3

Fig. 4

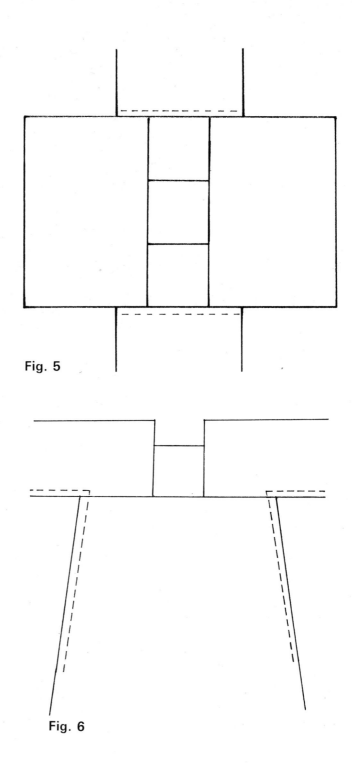

Fig. 5

Fig. 6

Burnouse

The burnouse, also spelt burnoose, burnous, or called 'capote' in North America, is a loose, pull-on type of garment with a hood. The body piece is wide and enveloping, and the sleeves are hardly more than cuffs. It is worn in the countries to the south and east of the Mediterranean Sea. The materials used are usually natural-coloured handspun and woven wools, in medium and heavy weights. See the colour photograph facing page 64.

Fabric requirements

There are several ways of cutting out a burnouse. The traditional method is to use only three pieces of fabric, but these have to be very carefully measured and cut, so that the hood and sleeve slits are correctly positioned. Other methods involve cutting more pieces of fabric, but the rectangular shapes are simpler and the fabric is used in a more economic manner.

A variety of widths of fabric can be used and as the garment is very loose, it will fit most adult sizes. Scale down for a child's size.

For layout A: 3 m (3¼ yds) of 90 cm (36″) fabric.
For layout B: 2·3 m (2½ yds) of 140 cm (54″) fabric.
For layout C: 2·3 m (2½ yds) of 140 cm (54″) fabric.

Suitable fabrics include all types of coating materials, wools, worsteds and blends, felts and blanket-type fabrics. They can be plain, textured, striped or checked. In no circumstances should fabrics with a one-way design or nap be used.

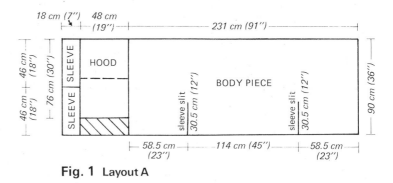

Fig. 1 Layout A

48

Serape/poncho constructed from two rectangles, worn with short semi-circular skirt. Fabric: hand-woven wool

Semicircular cloak with hood. Fabric: Welsh wool reversible double cloth. Edges and seams bound with braid

Poncho constructed from four rectangles; contrasting side pieces with plain insets. Fabric: hand-woven wool

Round-necked blouse smock, from three rectangles. Fabric: white muslin embroidered with multi-coloured cottons

Adaptation of 'round' smock constructed from rectangles. Fabric: square-weave cotton

Making up

Layout A

Lay out fabric as shown in Fig. 1 and cut out the pieces.

Fold hood in half and, with right sides together, stitch top edge (Fig. 2). Fold body piece along the sleeve slits (Fig. 3). Pin fronts of hood to fronts of body piece and pin centre backs of hood and body piece. Stitch hood from back to front along shoulder seams, until all of the hood is securely joined to body piece. Stitch remaining shoulder seams from hood to sleeve slits (Fig. 4).

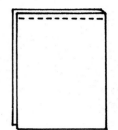

Fig. 2

Fig. 3

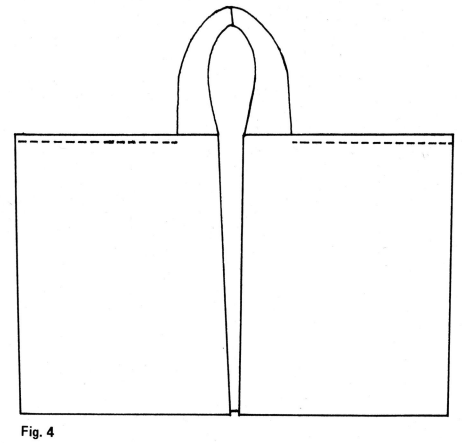

Fig. 4

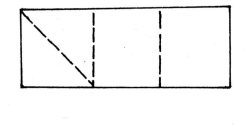

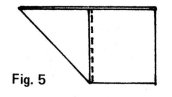

Fig. 5

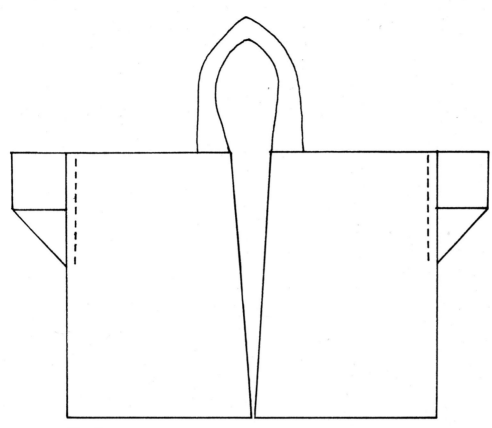

Fig. 6

Fold each sleeve piece into three. To make the gussets open up one-third of sleeve piece and fold diagonally as shown in Fig. 5. Stitch gusset in place (Fig. 5). Hem the hand opening. Insert sleeve into sleeve slit and stitch (Fig. 6).

Stitch centre front seam of body piece to within 20 cm (8″) of neck opening. Turn back and hem these 20 cm (8″) on each side of centre front and also turn back and hem front edges of hood (Fig. 7). The front opening can be fastened with a button and loop, or ties.

Turn up hem edge and stitch.

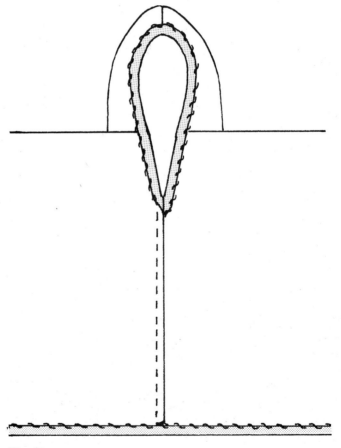

Fig. 7

Burnouse: all
seams were stitched
to the outside
and neatened by
herringbone stitch.

Layout B

Lay out fabric as shown in Fig. 8 and cut out the pieces. The main differences between this layout and the one shown in Fig. 1 are that there are no shoulder seams and the sleeve slits are replaced by full side seams.

Fold hood in half and, with right sides together, stitch top edge.

Fold body piece in half and match centre fronts and backs of hood and body piece. Stitch hood to body piece, easing the hood into neck slit.

Make sleeves as for layout A. Position and pin sleeves to tops of sides and stitch. Stitch remaining side seams.

Stitch centre front seam of body piece and neaten front opening and hood as for layout A. Attach a suitable fastening to front opening.

Turn up hem edge and stitch.

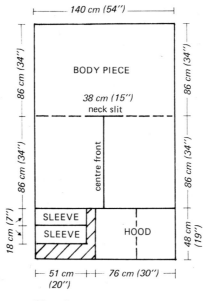

Fig. 8 Layout B

Layout C

This is the traditional method of cutting out a burnouse.

Lay out fabric as shown in Fig. 9 and cut out the pieces.

Stitch centre front seam of body section to within 20 cm (8″) of neck opening. With right sides together, position and stitch front edges of hood to centre front top edges of body section. Stitch remaining shoulder seams as for layout A.

With right sides together, stitch top edges of hood. Turn back centre front opening and front edges of hood and hem. Fasten front opening as for layouts A and B.

Make sleeves as for layout A. Insert sleeves into sleeve slits as for layout A and stitch.

Turn up hem edge and stitch.

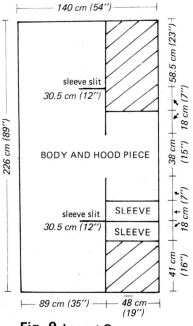

Fig. 9 Layout C

Coat with hood

This garment is made up from rectangular pieces of fabric and can be adapted to a short or long length, with short or long sleeves. It is cut from a variety of fabric widths.

Fabric requirements

The cutting layouts shown (Figs 1, 2 and 3) are for an average adult and use the widths most suited to economy of fabric. All these are adaptable to your own requirements.

For a knee-length coat with long sleeves: 3·7 m (4 yds) of 61 cm (24″) fabric, or approximately 1·8 m (2 yds) of 120 cm (48″) or 140 cm (54″) fabric.
For a long coat with long sleeves: 2·7 m (3 yds) of 90 cm (36″) fabric. Note that on this layout (Fig. 3) each sleeve is cut in two pieces.

Avoid using fabrics with a one-way design or nap on those cutting layouts where the hood and sleeves do not lie in the same direction. Striped fabrics can be used, but remember that if the stripes are running from neck to hem on body pieces, they will not run down the length of the sleeve, but *across* the width. Similarly, if the stripes are running across the body pieces, they will run *down* the sleeves. Otherwise, all types of fabrics are suitable, though a loosely knitted fabric may stretch if used for the full-length coat.

Making up

Lay out fabric, adapted to your requirements if necessary, as shown in Figs 1, 2 or 3. Calculate the neckline as shown on page 30. Cut out the pieces.

Figs 4 and 5 show an alternative hood with a gusset. This can be cut out in one piece (Fig. 5), or, possibly more economically, in three pieces (Fig. 4).

Join shoulder seams (Fig. 6). If necessary, join sleeves for 'overarm' seam (Fig. 6). Match centre points of sleeves and shoulder seams and stitch sleeves to body (Figs 6 and 7). Join underarm and side seams (Fig. 8).

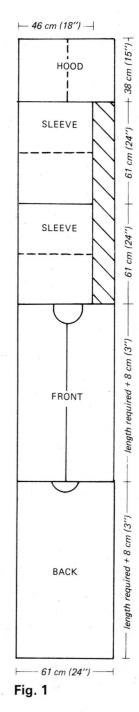

Fig. 1

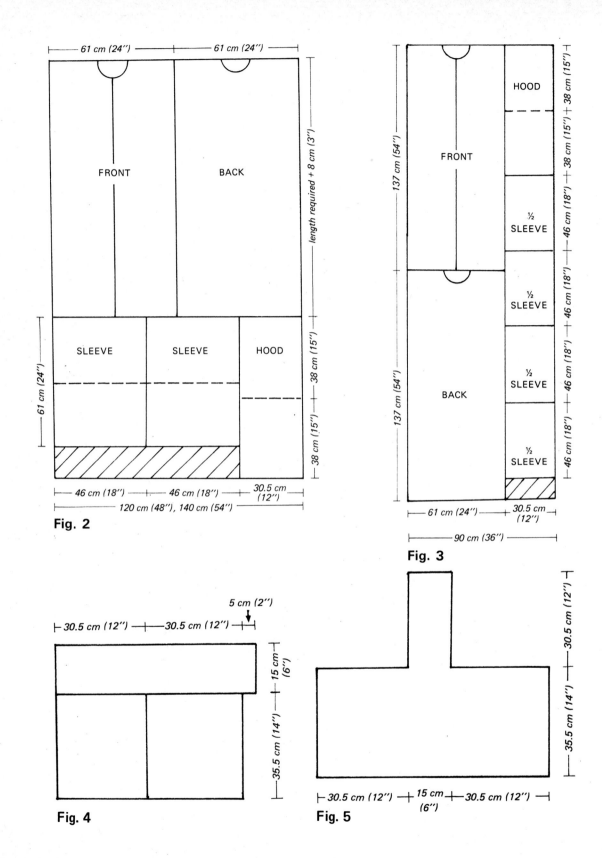

├── 61 cm (24″) ──┤── 61 cm (24″) ──┤

FRONT

BACK

length required + 8 cm (3″)

61 cm (24″)

38 cm (15″)

SLEEVE

SLEEVE

HOOD

38 cm (15″)

├── 46 cm (18″) ──┤── 46 cm (18″) ──┤ 30.5 cm (12″)
├──────── 120 cm (48″), 140 cm (54″) ────────┤

Fig. 2

137 cm (54″)

FRONT

HOOD

38 cm (15″)

38 cm (15″)

½ SLEEVE

46 cm (18″)

½ SLEEVE

46 cm (18″)

137 cm (54″)

BACK

½ SLEEVE

46 cm (18″)

½ SLEEVE

46 cm (18″)

├── 61 cm (24″) ──┤ 30.5 cm (12″)
├──────── 90 cm (36″) ────────┤

Fig. 3

5 cm (2″)
├ 30.5 cm (12″) ┤ 30.5 cm (12″) ┤

15 cm (6″)

35.5 cm (14″)

Fig. 4

30.5 cm (12″)

35.5 cm (14″)

├ 30.5 cm (12″) ┤ 15 cm (6″) ┤ 30.5 cm (12″) ┤

Fig. 5

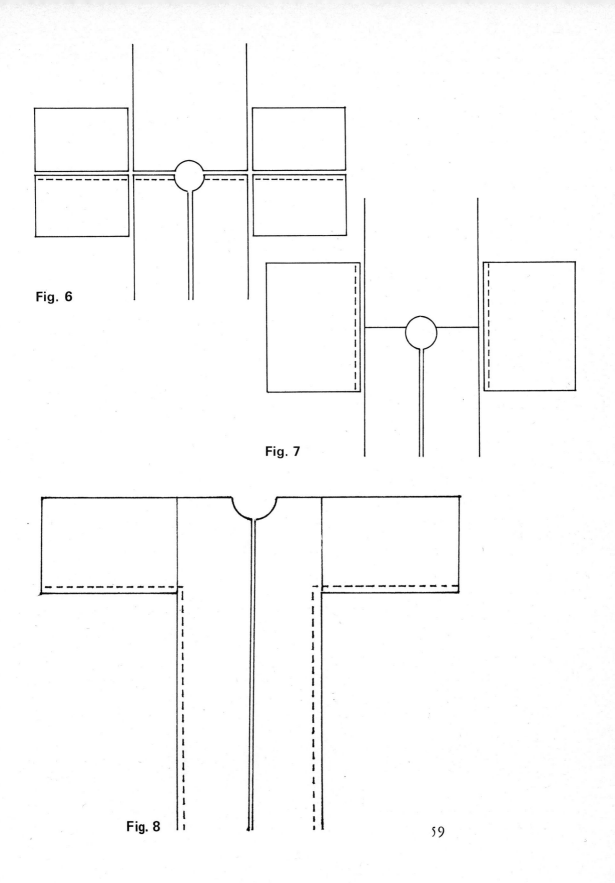

Fig. 6

Fig. 7

Fig. 8

With right sides together, stitch top and back seams of hood (Fig. 9). If hood is cut in one piece, fold fabric with right sides together and stitch one side (Fig. 10). Clip point at top of hood. The alternative hood shown in Figs 4 and 5 is made up with the long rectangle stitched between the two side pieces to form a box-like head covering (Fig. 11).

With right sides together, match centre backs of hood and body of coat. Pin hood round neck opening; the front points of hood and coat should meet at the two centre fronts. Stitch hood in position.

The front opening may be finished in several ways. Turn back centre front edges and front edge of hood and hem (Fig. 12). A firmer edge can be achieved by attaching a facing along both front edges and round hood opening (Fig. 13).

To fasten coat, attach a hemmed strip round front opening and hood (Fig. 14). The completed width of the strip should be 2·5 cm–5 cm (1″–2″). Firmly hem strip to edge of coat, leaving spaces for buttonholes. Stitch buttons to strip on one side and fasten coat by buttoning into the unsewn gaps on the other side (Fig. 14).

Rouleau button loops can be inserted to project between the facing and coat edge (Fig. 15 and see page 157). The coat is then fastened by these button loops and buttons.

Alternatively, attach ties, or hooks and eyes, down front opening (Fig. 16).

Turn up sleeves and lower edge to desired lengths and stitch.

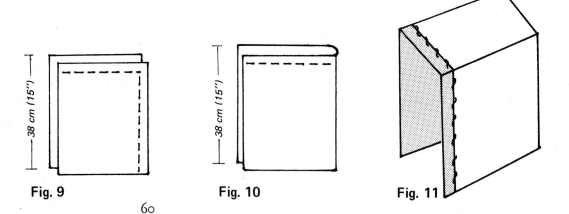

Fig. 9   Fig. 10   Fig. 11

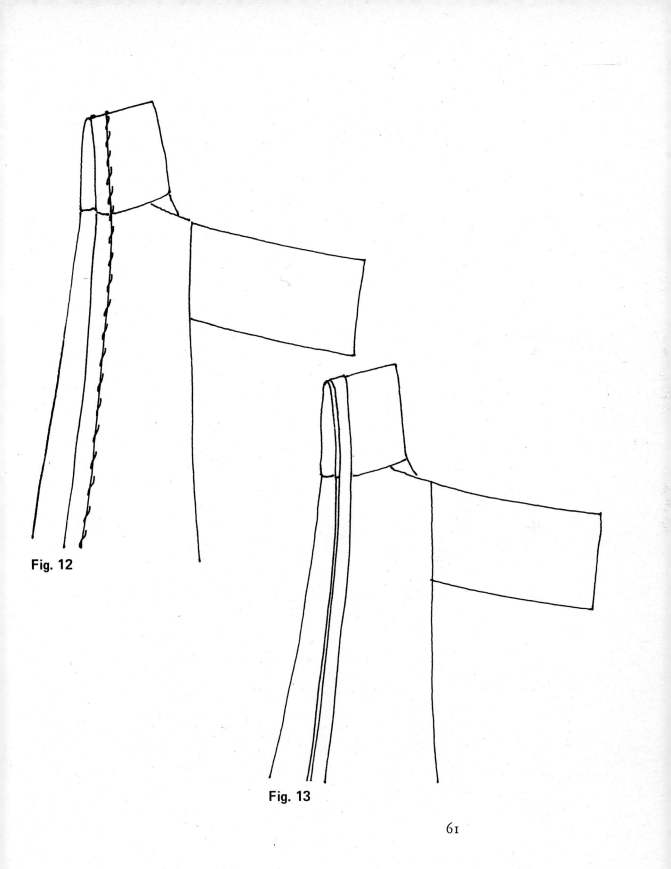

Fig. 12

Fig. 13

61

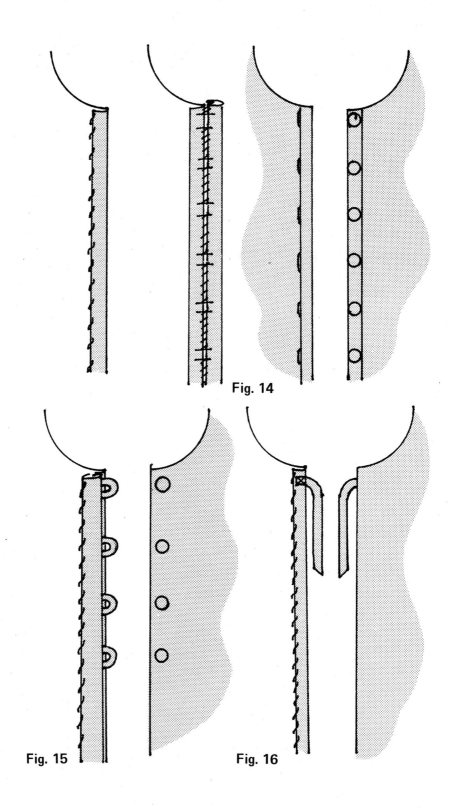

Fig. 14

Fig. 15

Fig. 16

Happi coat

This coat or jacket is based on the style of the Eastern 'happi' coats, which have wide sleeves and are tightly wrapped and tied round the body. The traditional cut of a happi coat is similar to the 'Coat with hood' on page 56, but with more wrapover of material in front and wider sleeves. The layouts shown here consist of three or four pieces and are very simple to make up. The garment is ideal as an 'at home' gown or casual jacket.

Fabric requirements

The long coat or short jacket can be cut from a variety of fabric widths.

For a short jacket: 2·4 m (2⅔ yds) of 90 cm (36″) fabric.
For a knee- or full-length coat: increase length on front and back pieces and use 90 cm (36″) fabric.

For 120 cm (48″), 140 cm (54″) and 150 cm (60″) fabric widths, the layout is constructed in a different way. The length of the coat is cut completely on the side (Fig. 2). The length of the coat is, therefore, determined by the width of the fabric. Regardless of the width used, 2·3 m (2½ yds) of fabric are required.

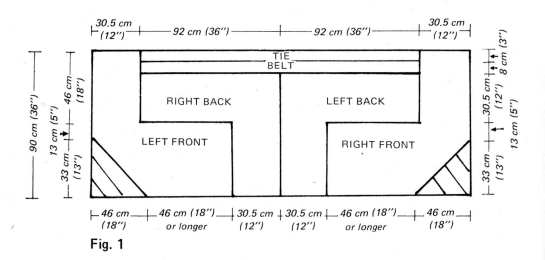

Fig. 1

64

Cover-up with a one-piece hood, constructed from four rectangles.
Fabric: machine-knitted tufted wool

Four-piece dress with self-bound edges.
Fabric: checked seersucker cotton

Tunic blouse, constructed from one piece of fabric, with a yoke.
Fabric: Indian seersucker furnishing cotton

Burnouse with the 'cuffs' cut in two pieces.
Fabric: hand-woven natural-coloured wools

Triangular top and tubular skirt. The top is sewn double to give vertical stripes, and the skirt is folded by the man's method. Fabric: diagonal-striped cotton

Many types of lightweight, mediumweight and heavyweight fabrics can be used. The luxurious Eastern coats were made of silk, while the utility Eastern coats were made of cotton, often quilted for warmth. Avoid using fabrics with a one-way design or nap.

Making up

Lay out fabric as shown in Figs 1 or 2 and cut out the pieces.

If using a 90 cm (36″) fabric, stitch centre back seam.

Stitch underarm and side seams (Fig. 3).

Pin shoulder seams. It may be necessary to take in any surplus fabric at the two centre fronts of the coat, so that the front lies flat across the chest (Fig. 4). Try on garment, make any necessary adjustments and stitch.

The bottom front edges of the coat may not line up with rest of hem. If so, level off front edges so that they line up (Fig. 5).

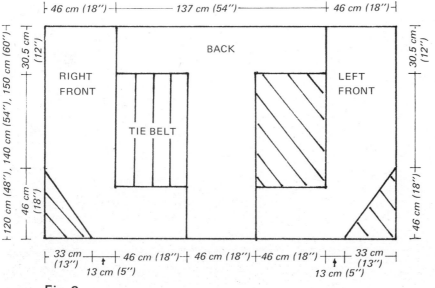

Fig. 2

Bind neckline with bias binding or tape (Fig. 5). Turn back all other edges and bind with bias binding or tape, or hem. The binding can form a decorative edging, or can be turned back completely to the wrong side.

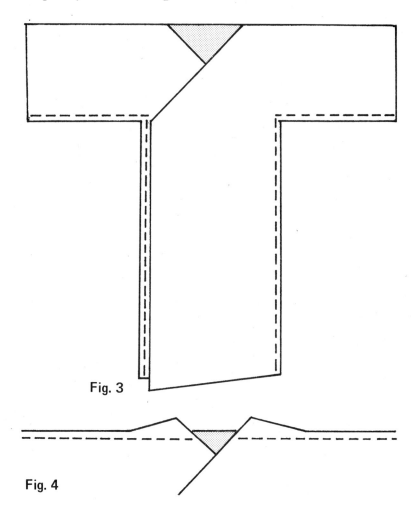

Fig. 3

Fig. 4

Make a tie belt cut from remaining fabric. The tie belt should be at least 1·8 m (72″) long and 10 cm (4″) wide. If fabric is not long enough, join pieces together until they form a long enough strip (Fig. 6). With wrong sides together, fold tie belt in half lengthways, turn in raw edges and hem or slipstitch edges together (Fig. 6).

66

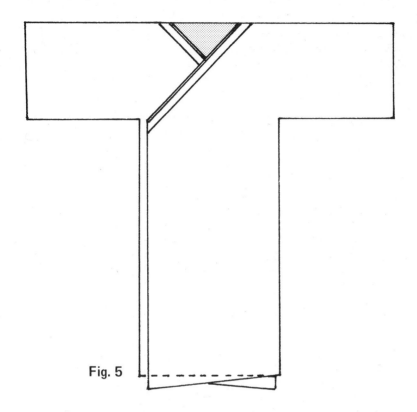

Fig. 5

The coat is worn with one front wrapped over the other and held in place by the waist tie belt. In Eastern countries, the left side is wrapped over the right side for either sex. The only time the right side is wrapped over the left, is in funeral gowns worn by the deceased.

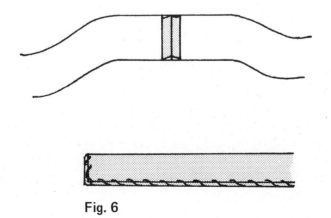

Fig. 6

Traditional smocks and their variations

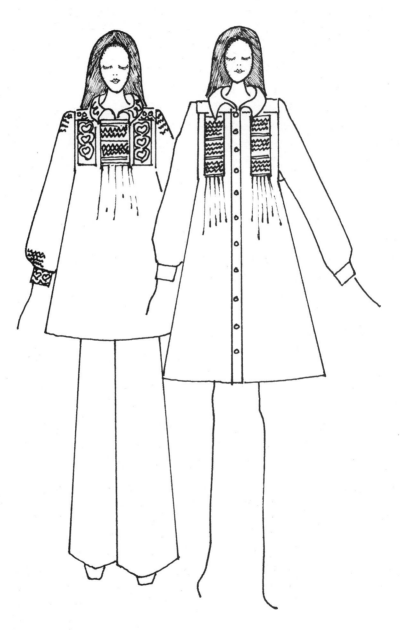

The English smock is a perfect example of a garment cut from rectangular and square pieces of material. The word 'smock' has an ancient derivation from the Anglo-Saxon meaning of shift or chemise, with the development from being a shift (a tight-fitting garment) to being the full smock of the country worker that allows ease of movement. Smocks reached the height of their popularity towards the end of the last century. Today we have a revival in loose-fitting smocks, but they are designed in a different way to the traditional ones.

The traditional smock was either reversible, with a similar design in embroidery and smocking stitches on the back and front of the garment; a small opening at the neck enabled the garment to be pulled over the head. Or, the smock had a buttoned front opening.

Many of the traditional smocks were planned in a very simple way. Three times the length from neck to hem was the amount of fabric required, which was then cut into three equal lengths. Two of these lengths were used for the front and back sections and the third length was used for the collar, yokes, cuffs and gussets. The width of fabric used was approximately 90 cm (36") and within this, the smocked area would take up three times its finished width.

A hard-wearing fabric was used, such as hemp, linen or cotton, and the surface embroidery and smocking were worked with linen or cotton thread. The first working smocks were adorned only with the basic smocking stitches, but later became covered with surface embroidery on the collar, yokes, 'boxes' (the areas alongside the gathers or 'tubing' on back and front of garment), and parts of the sleeves. The amount of surface embroidery increased with the rise in popularity of the smock.

The embroidery was often built up of circles, spirals and straight lines, becoming abstractly floral within the potential of the stitches used.

Colours of the smocks varied from county to county, but, generally, the everyday working smock was of a drab colour, from cream to black, with toning or contrasting stitchery. Sunday smocks were white with self-coloured stitchery.

Variation of a traditional smock. The natural-coloured cotton used for this smock is embroidered with cotton thread of a darker tone.

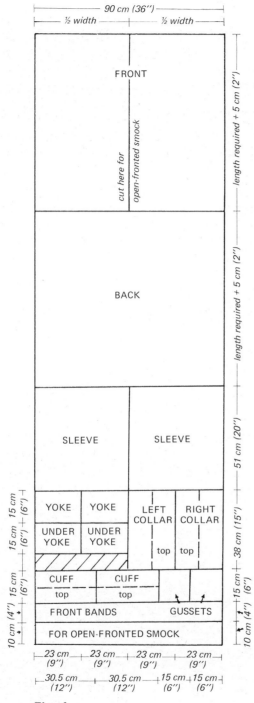

Fig. 1

Fabric requirements

Traditional smocks can be divided into two styles, (*a*) front and back identical, and (*b*) buttoned front opening.

For an average adult: 3·4 m (3⅔ yds) of 90 cm (36″) fabric are required for a knee-length smock.

The layout shown in Fig. 1 is easily adaptable to different sizes and widths of fabric.

As a lot of work can be put into the stitchery of a smock, the most suitable fabric to use is a plain, high-quality cotton or linen. A cotton and man-made fibre blend is also suitable.

Making up

Lay out fabric as shown in Fig. 1, or as adapted to your own requirements. Cut out the pieces. All seam allowances are 2·5 cm (1″) and these are included in the dimensions given in the layout. Additional instructions for making the open-fronted smock will be found at the end of this section.

Before making up the smock, the gathers, or tubing, must be prepared and all the smocking and embroidery must be worked. A smock can be made without any embroidery or smocking; stitched tucks can take the place of smocking

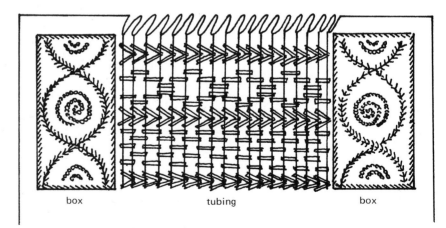

box   tubing   box

Fig. 2

stitches, or the gathers can be in the form of machined elastic thread. However, the traditional smocking retains a certain amount of elasticity and greatly adds to the look and comfort of the garment.

The parts of the garment chosen for embroidery should be worked first, starting with the boxes (the areas alongside the gathers or tubing). The widths of these boxes are from 8 cm–15 cm (3″–6″) and the length of the embroidery is usually worked to line up with the underarm seam (Fig. 2). The embroidery stitches used on traditional smocks are all types of feather stitchery, chain, stem and satin stitches, and french knots (Fig. 3).

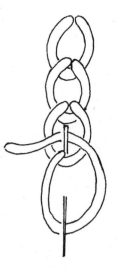

Fig. 3a Chain stitch

Progressive developments of feather stitch

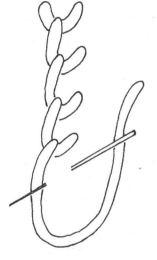

Figs. 3b   3c   3d

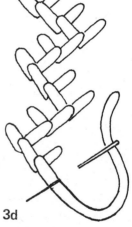

Fig. 3e Satin stitch   **Fig. 3f** French knot

73

For the collar, cuffs and yokes, embroider one layer of fabric only, so that when the smock is made up, the back of the stitchery will be neatly concealed.

The tubing, or gathers, is the central area of a smock, which is gathered up to control the fullness of the garment. This stage must be worked with great care. The gathering threads should run from right to left, each stitch set directly under the same stitch in the row above, and the rows of stitching should all be the same distance apart. The stitches should not be more than 1 cm ($\frac{1}{2}$") apart or in length (Fig. 4). Start each line of gathers with a knotted thread and sew for the required distance. Work the required number of rows, including one extra row at top and bottom of the tubing. These extra rows counteract the flare of the fabric when working the stitchery on the tubing. Draw up the gathering threads and tie off securely (Fig. 5). The area is now ready for the smocking embellishment.

The smocking stitchery should be worked from left to right along the tubing and should be kept level along the gathers. The basic stitch is called rope, or stem, and combinations of this stitch with variations make up the smocked area. Some of the variations are called basket, or cable, and chevron, or wave

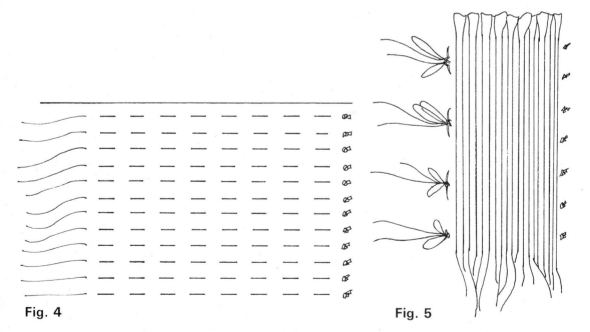

Fig. 4   Fig. 5

(Figs 6 and 7). Always finish the top and bottom of the smocking area with a row of rope (stem) stitch to strengthen the gathers.

When the smocking stitchery is completed, the gathering threads can be removed. If the fullness at either the top or bottom of the sleeves is to be smocked, this can be worked now before the sleeves are joined to the body, or the cuffs attached to the sleeves.

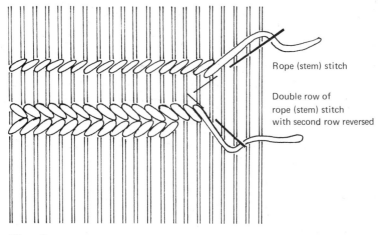

Rope (stem) stitch

Double row of
rope (stem) stitch
with second row reversed

Fig. 6

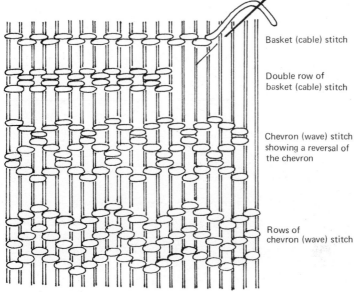

Basket (cable) stitch

Double row of
basket (cable) stitch

Chevron (wave) stitch
showing a reversal of
the chevron

Rows of
chevron (wave) stitch

Fig. 7

After completing all the embroidery and smocking, the garment is ready to be made up.

Place the embroidered, or top, yokes lengthways between back and front pieces and stitch (Fig. 8).

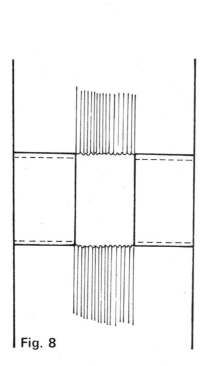

Fig. 8

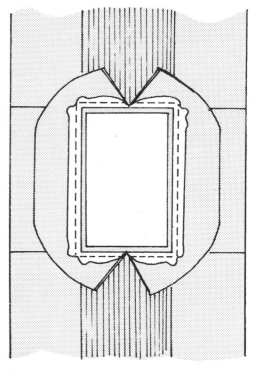

Fig. 9

Fold collar pieces in half and stitch short ends together. Take the edge of the non-embroidered, or bottom, half of one collar piece and, with right sides together, tack collar to neck edge. Start at centre front and work towards centre back. Tack on the other collar piece in the same way. The collar pieces should meet at centre front and back. Stitch collar pieces to neck edge (Fig. 9). Fold each collar over so that the embroidery is lying on top of the collar, turn in the raw edges and slipstitch to wrong side of neck edge (Fig. 10).

Stitch sleeve seams, leaving 10 cm (4″) open at top of underarm seams for the gussets.

76

To make up cuffs follow instructions for making the shirt cuffs on pages 96 and 102. Or make a closed cuff, which is just wide enough for the hand to pass through.

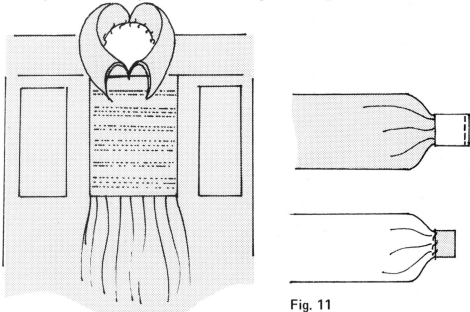

Fig. 10

Fig. 11

With right sides together, stitch short ends of cuffs. Turn right side out. Gather up sleeves to same width as cuff bands. If the base of each sleeve has been smocked, gathering may not be necessary. Stitch cuff bands to sleeves (Fig. 11). Turn in raw edges and slipstitch to wrong side of sleeves (Fig. 11).

With right sides together, match the centre points of sleeves and yokes. Pin sleeves to body and stitch (Fig. 12). Stitch side seams, leaving 10 cm (4″) unstitched below sleeve and body join.

Pin and tack gussets into the squares left under the arms of the smock. There are three ways of stitching the gussets in place.

1 Turn smock inside out. Pin and tack each gusset with its right side down into the square left in the underarm and side seams. Hand-stitch through gusset and seams so that the stitching is invisible from the right side (Fig. 13).

2 Position gusset as above. Turn smock right side out and slipstitch gusset in place (Fig. 14).

77

3 Turn in the four edges of the gusset and press. Place gusset right side up on the outer side of the smock, like a patch. Pin in position and stitch. This is probably the simplest method of attaching the gusset. It will look like the previous method (Fig. 14), but it will be a little more bulky because of the turned edges and corners of the gusset.

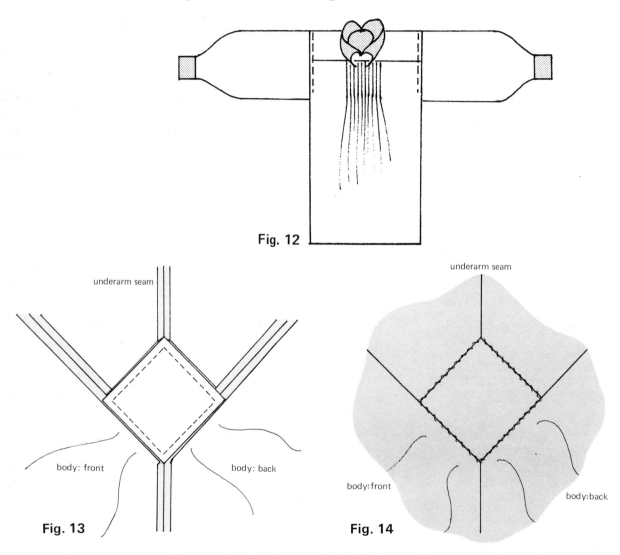

Fig. 12

underarm seam

body: front

body: back

Fig. 13

underarm seam

body: front

body: back

Fig. 14

Fig. 15 shows the smock inside out with gussets stitched in place.

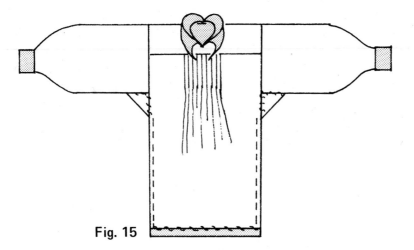

Fig. 15

Stitch under yokes to wrong sides of top yokes.

Turn up lower edge of smock and stitch.

OPEN-FRONTED SMOCK

The following are additional instructions for the open-fronted smock.

Lay out fabric as shown in Fig. 1, but cut the front piece in half as shown. Cut out all pieces.

Follow the instructions given for the reversible smock, except for the front of the garment. The front of the buttoned smock is in two sections and the tubing, or gathers, is on both sides of the opening. Embroidery can be worked on either side of the tubing.

The front button bands are made up after the stitchery has been completed. Fold bands in half lengthways. For the button side of front opening, take one band and, with right sides together, stitch band to one side of front opening. Turn in raw edge of band and hem to wrong side of garment.

For the buttonhole side of front opening, take the other band and, with right sides together, stitch to other side of front opening. Make the required number of buttonholes. Alternatively, when stitching buttonhole band to front opening, leave an appropriate number of spaces in the seam for the button-holes. Turn in raw edge of band and hem to wrong side of garment, matching the spaces left for the buttonholes in the seam. In this way, the buttonholes are formed between the band and body of the smock (see page 62).

The collar is made up in the same way as the reversible smock, but it meets at the front at the centre points of both button bands.

VARIATIONS OF TRADITIONAL SMOCKS

The illustration opposite shows just three examples. On the left, the collar of the smock has been enlarged to form a shoulder cape, which is cut from a semicircle of fabric. This type of smock is open-fronted and, if made in a heavyweight fabric, it would make an attractive coat. Stitched tucks and pleating replace the more usual tubing or gathers.

The centre smock is constructed in a similar way to the traditional smock, but without the collar. Tucks at the sides of front and back of body piece control the fullness and the centre panel can be embroidered or left plain. The sleeves are not attached to cuffs, but are allowed to hang freely.

The smock on the right is also constructed in a similar way to the traditional smock, but the smocking and embroidery are taken to waist level and the length of the smock is extended to the ground.

Many other variations are possible, while still keeping the construction to varying sizes of rectangles. Changes can be made in the positioning of the tubing or tucks, and the amount of surface embroidery. Experiments can be carried out on different types of fabrics, from the traditional plain fabrics and colours, to the wide range of modern fabrics now available.

Round-necked blouse smock

A peasant blouse with a gathered rounded neck is found throughout Europe, Russia, Scandinavia, and South and Central America. Traditionally, the blouse was made in white fabric, usually linen, but now cotton fabrics are used. The top part of the body and sleeves are embellished with colourful embroidery. See the colour photograph facing page 49.

Fabric requirements

The garment consists of one rectangle for the body piece, with two sleeve slits cut into it; two squares for the sleeves and two small squares for the underarm gussets. The gathering at the neck and sleeves gives the garment its form.

For long sleeves: 1·2 m (1⅓ yds) of 140 cm (54″) fabric.
For short sleeves: 0·9 m (1 yd) of 140 cm (54″) fabric.
The same length of 120 cm (48″) fabric can also be used, but the garment will not be as full, and 8 cm (3″) must be added on for the two gussets.

If using the traditional cutting method for a 90 cm (36″) fabric, there is a lot of wastage and 2·6 m (2⅞ yds) are required for a long-sleeved blouse, or 2 m (2⅙ yds) for a short-sleeved blouse (Fig. 2). However, a less wasteful layout can be planned by cutting the body piece of the blouse in three, thus having two additional seams, but requiring only 1·8 m (2 yds) of 90 cm (36″) fabric for a long-sleeved blouse (Fig. 3); or 1·4 m (1½ yds) for a short-sleeved blouse (Fig. 4).

All types of lightweight fabrics can be used, but if embroidery is to be worked on the garment, it is advisable to choose a natural-coloured fabric.

Making up

Lay out fabric as shown in Figs 1, 2, 3 or 4 and cut out the pieces.

If embroidery is to be worked on the blouse, this can be done before making up, or after stitching sleeves in position, but before gathering neck or sleeves. The traditional embroidery motifs are floral, and geometric combinations of lines and dots.

The stitches used can be simple, such as satin, chain and cross stitch, or the embroidery can be developed using a wider range of stitches.

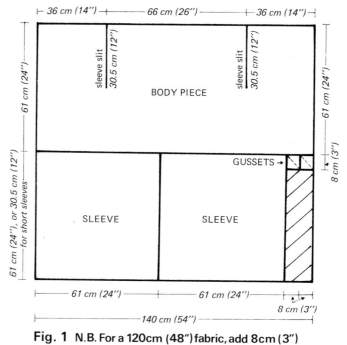

Fig. 1 N.B. For a 120cm (48") fabric, add 8cm (3") for gussets.

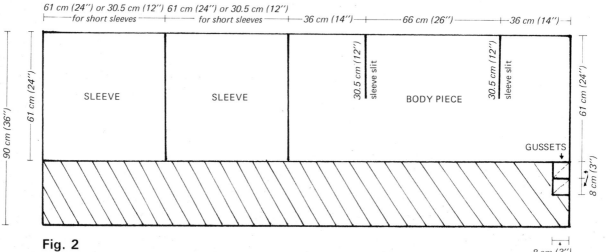

Fig. 2

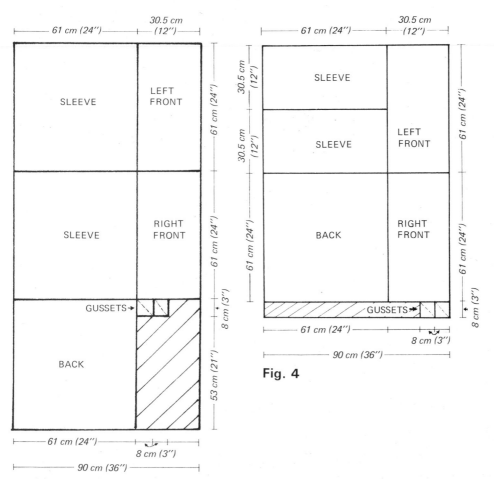

Fig. 3

Fig. 4

For each sleeve, pin and stitch underarm seam, leaving 8 cm (3″) open at the body end. Fold gusset piece in half diagonally as shown on the layouts. Pin and hand-stitch gusset to each side of the underarm seam (Fig. 5). The gusset only needs 1 cm (½″) turnings. Or attach gussets later, as in 'Traditional smocks' (p. 78).

If using the layout in Figs 3 or 4, stitch fronts to back, leaving 30·5 cm (12″) open at top of body piece for insertion of sleeves.

Pin and stitch sleeves, with gussets, into sleeve slits. The sleeves will extend a little way beyond the top of the slits (Fig. 6).

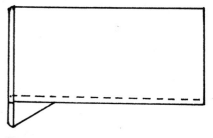

Fig. 5

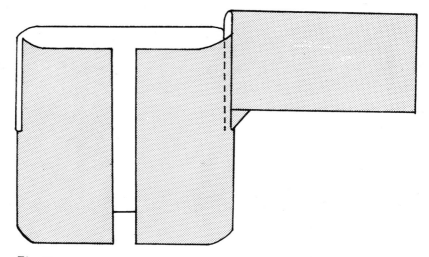

Fig. 6

Turn in 1 cm (½″) on centre front openings, lower edges of sleeves and body, and stitch. The front is fastened by hooks and eyes, or small buttons and button loops.

Using small running stitches, run a row of gathering round the neckline (Fig. 7) and draw up to required size. Tie off gathering thread. Bind neckline with narrow straight tape to hold gathers in place (Fig. 8).

The gathers at the wrists may be worked in various ways. Using small running stitches, work one row of gathering 2·5 cm (1″) from the hemmed edge of each sleeve and draw up gathers to fit, allowing enough room for entry of hand (Fig. 9). Secure gathering with narrow straight tape stitched over the gathering thread.

86

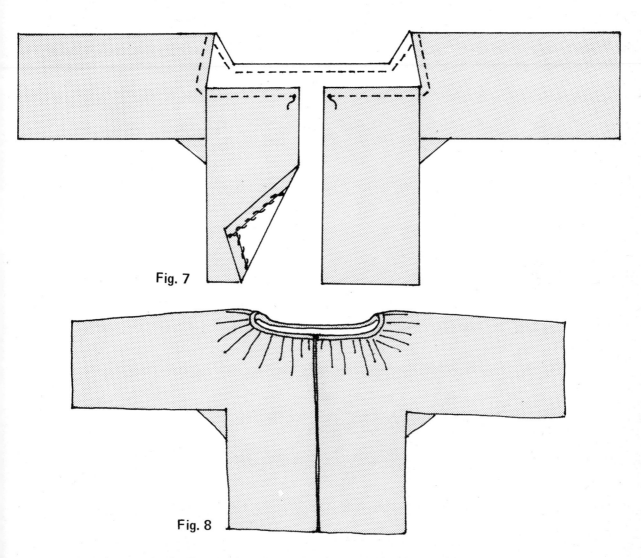

Fig. 7

Fig. 8

Another method of gathering the wrists is to stitch tape to the wrong side of sleeves 2·5 cm (1″) from hemmed edges. Leave an opening where tape ends overlap. Insert elastic through tape channel and stitch ends of elastic securely together.

Alternatively, the wrists can be finished by embroidering a band of cross stitch 2·5 cm (1″) from hemmed edge of each sleeve (Fig. 10). Thread a cord under the stitches, pull up cord to required width and tie. The cord can be loosened for easier laundering.

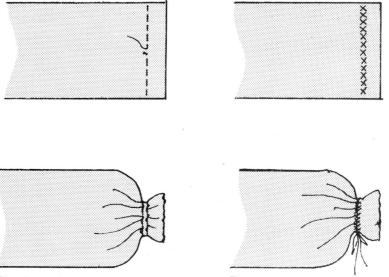

Fig. 9   Fig. 10

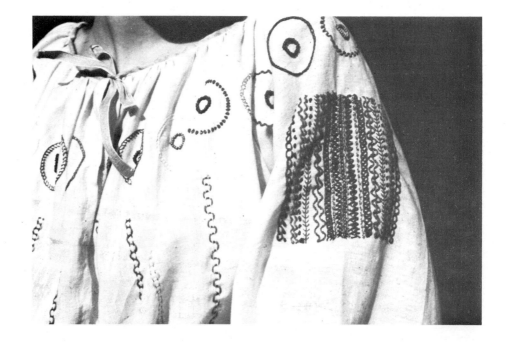

*Detail of
round-necked
blouse smock*

Square-necked blouse smock

This type of smock has developed from many cultures, and is still a popular garment in South America. The fabric is usually white muslin and embroidery is worked on the yoke and sleeves. The bottoms of the sleeves are gathered by threading a cord through a row of cross stitch.

Fabric requirements

For short sleeves: 1·6 m (1¾ yds) of 90 cm (36″) fabric, or 1·4 m (1½ yds) of 120 cm (48″) fabric.
For long sleeves: 1·6 m (1¾ yds) of 120 cm (48″) fabric.

Any plain fabric is suitable, or one with a small and delicate non-directional pattern.

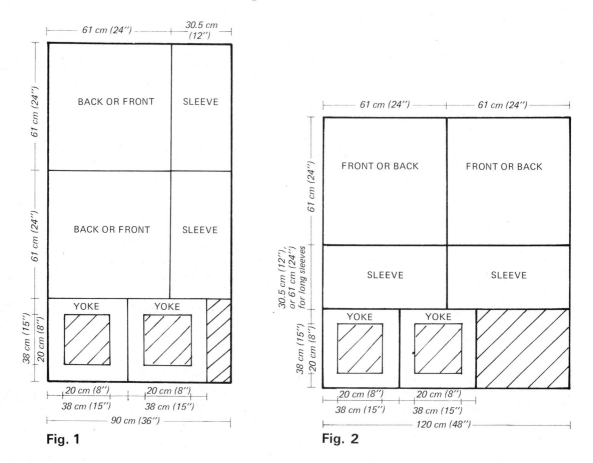

Fig. 1

Fig. 2

Square-necked blouse smock made in cotton lawn, worn with a wrap-around skirt made in Indian furnishing cotton.

Making up

Lay out fabric as shown in Figs 1 or 2 and cut out the pieces.

Work the embroidery on one yoke piece, tops of back, front and sleeves if required. Hem the bottoms of the sleeves and work a row of cross stitch 2·5 cm (1″) from each hemmed edge (see page 88).

Stitch side seams of body, leaving 8 cm (3″) open at top of seams. Stitch sleeve seams, again leaving 8 cm (3″) open at top of seams (Fig. 3). Clip diagonally across the 8 cm (3″) at tops of body and sleeves (Fig. 3). Join body and sleeves together at the 8 cm (3″) cut edges (Fig. 4).

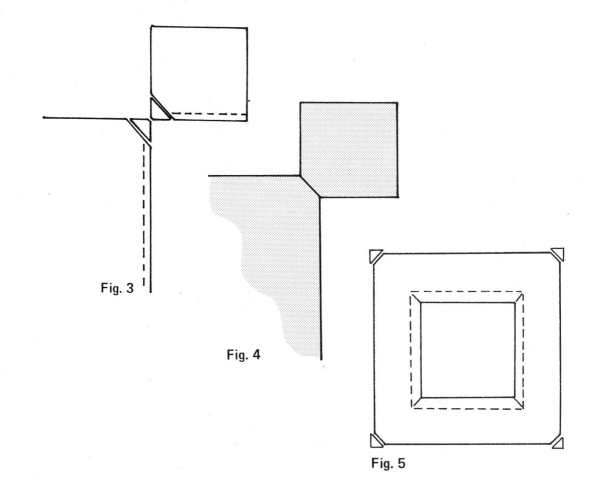

Fig. 3

Fig. 4

Fig. 5

With right sides together, stitch the two yoke pieces round the four inner edges of the square (Fig. 5). Clip all corners and turn right side out. Turn in raw edges on both yoke pieces to wrong side, press and make sure that yoke lies flat.

Using small running stitches, run a row of gathering all the way round top of body sections and sleeves (Fig. 6). Draw up gathering thread to fit into yoke.

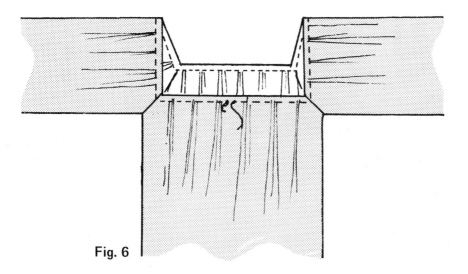

Fig. 6

Pin gathered body piece to yoke, spreading gathers evenly all round the sides of yoke. The back, front and each sleeve should each have one side of the yoke. Hemming stitch yoke to body on right and wrong sides of garment (Figs 7 and 8).

Turn up lower edge of blouse and stitch. Thread a brightly coloured cord under the row of cross stitch on each sleeve. Pull up to required width and tie.

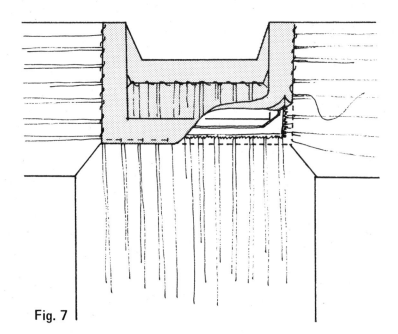

Fig. 7

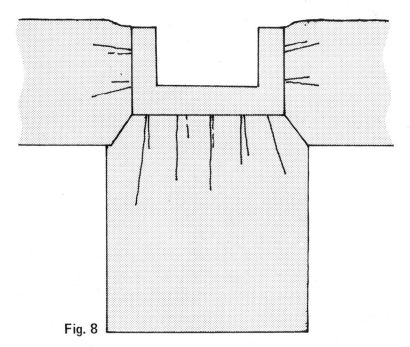

Fig. 8

This shirt is of a very simple cut and can be pulled on over the head. Embroidery on the collar, cuffs and round the front opening was worked on this type of shirt in Scandinavia. The material used traditionally was natural linen and the embroidery was worked in bright colours.

Fabric requirements

The shirt consists of rectangular pieces of fabric, with the possible addition of a shaped front panel. The shirt is intended to be loose-fitting and the layout shown in Fig. 1 will fit a man, sizes 97 cm–107 cm (38″–42″) chest.

For a man's shirt: 2·1 m (2⅓ yds) of 90 cm (36″) fabric.

To adapt the layout for a woman, cut a smaller body rectangle, for example, 56 cm × 140 cm (22″ × 55″), and reduce the length of sleeves, collar and cuffs. This adapted layout would be suitable for sizes 86 cm–97 cm (34″–38″) bust.

For a woman's shirt: 1·6 m (1¾ yds) of 90 cm (36″) fabric.

All types of shirting fabrics are suitable, from fine cottons and lightweight wools and blends, to heavyweight fabrics for overshirts. Woven and jersey fabrics are also suitable. Avoid using fabrics with a one-way design or nap.

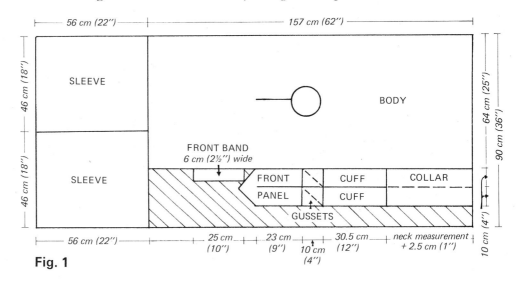

Fig. 1

96

Making up

See page 30 for instructions on calculating necklines. Lay out fabric as shown in Fig. 1 and cut out the pieces.

If the shirt is to be embroidered, it is easier to work this before stitching. Alternatively, the embroidery could be left until the shirt is made up.

Fold the collar piece in half, right sides together, and stitch the short ends (Fig. 2). Turn right side out and turn raw edges to wrong side (Fig. 3). Turn front opening edges 1 cm ($\frac{1}{2}''$) to wrong side (Fig. 4). With right sides together, pin bottom part of collar to neck opening, making sure that the fronts of the collar come to the edges of the front opening. Stitch collar to neck opening 1 cm ($\frac{1}{2}''$) from edge (Fig. 4). Trim seam to 6 mm ($\frac{1}{4}''$) and clip curve to help collar sit well. Turn in raw edge of collar 1 cm ($\frac{1}{2}''$) and stitch to wrong side of neck (Fig. 5).

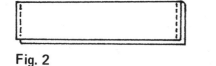

Fig. 2

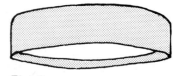

Fig. 3

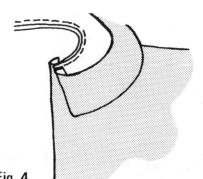

Fig. 4

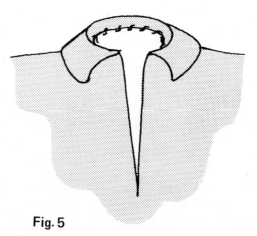

Fig. 5

Shirt made in a wool and cotton blend, with a topstitched front panel and quilted collar and cuffs.

If using the front opening band, attach it to right-hand side of opening for men and to left-hand side of opening for women. With right sides together, stitch raw edge of band to one turned-back edge of front opening, with 1 cm ($\frac{1}{2}$") seam. Turn in short edges of band and stitch ends. Stitch other long edge of band to wrong side of front opening (Fig. 6).

If using the front panel, turn all raw edges to wrong side. With wrong side of front panel facing right side of garment, pin panel to front and stitch in place (Fig. 7).   '

To close front opening, sew on press studs, hooks and eyes, or other suitable fastening. Sew one part of the fastening to the front opening band and the other part to the opposing front side, so that the openings lie flat together. Buttonholes could be worked through the front panel and buttons attached to the front band.

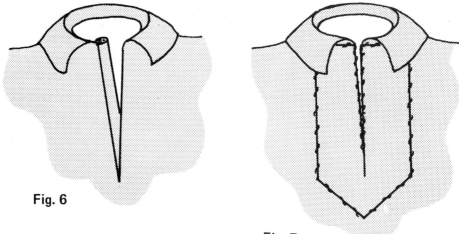

Fig. 6

Fig. 7

It is possible to make the shirt without a front panel or band, if the only closing of the neck is by ties. However, if the shirt is to be closed at the neck, then it is necessary to attach the front band for a flat well-fitting fastening. The addition of the front panel adds strength and decoration to the front opening.

Run a row of gathering at shoulder edge of sleeves (Fig. 8). Draw up gathering thread 5 cm (2") on shoulder edge, positioning the gathers at top of shoulder (Fig. 9). The shoulders of the sleeves can be sewn flat, without gathers, to the body piece.

With right sides together, stitch sleeves to body (Fig. 10). Note that the garment is still in a flat form at this stage.

Stitch underarm seams of sleeves, leaving 8 cm (3″) open at underarm join for gusset and 8 cm (3″) open at cuff end (Fig. 11). Stitch side seams of body, again leaving 8 cm (3″) open at underarm join for gusset (Fig. 11). The bottom 8 cm (3″) of the side seams may also be left open, as is often found in men's shirts.

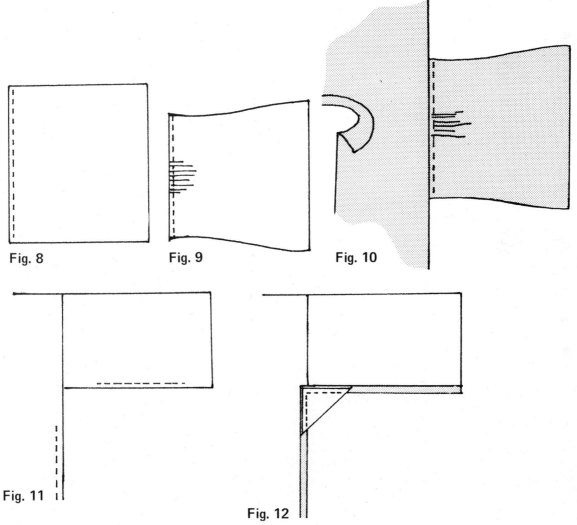

Fig. 8

Fig. 9

Fig. 10

Fig. 11

Fig. 12

Fig. 13

Fold each gusset piece in half diagonally as shown on the layout. Pin and stitch each gusset to right sides of underarm and side seams (Fig. 12).

Fold each cuff piece in half, right sides together, and stitch ends, allowing 1 cm ($\frac{1}{2}''$) seam and stopping 1 cm ($\frac{1}{2}''$) from long edge (Fig. 13). Turn right side out.

Make a gather round cuff edge of each sleeve and draw up to required width, so that it will fit round arm with a little ease for movement. With right sides together, pin each cuff to sleeves, leaving an overlap at one side of cuff. Make sure that this overlap will lap the sleeve correctly for each arm (Fig. 14). Stitch cuffs to sleeves and trim off any excess fabric. Turn in raw edges and slipstitch to the wrong side of sleeves over the first sewing line. Slipstitch sleeve opening (Fig. 15).

The cuffs may be fastened by press studs, or buttons and buttonholes.

Hem lower edge of shirt and side slits.

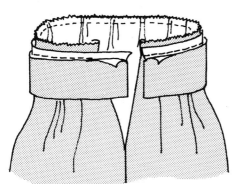

Fig. 14

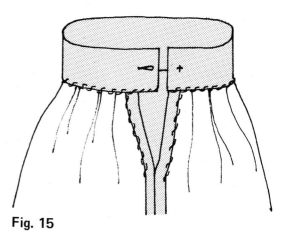

Fig. 15

Tunic blouse

One piece of fabric is the basis for this blouse and it is cut with a slight flare in the body to give a more graceful line. The neck opening is cut just large enough to allow for head entry. Two more pieces of fabric are required, for the yoke, to finish the neckline. See the colour photograph facing page 64.

Fabric requirements

For long sleeves: 1·5 m (1⅔ yds) of 140 cm (54″) fabric.
For short sleeves: 1·5 m (1⅔ yds) of 90 cm (36″) fabric plus bias binding for neck opening. Or 1·8 m (2 yds) of 90 cm (36″) fabric to allow for cutting a yoke.

Most fabrics are suitable and can be plain, striped, or with a non-directional pattern. Fabrics with a one-way design or nap can be used, but this means making 'shoulder' seams.

Making up

Fold fabric in half right sides together. Calculate neckline of yoke as shown on page 30; the thickness of the yoke should be 8 cm (3″). Lay out fabric as shown in Figs 1 or 2 and cut out

N.B. A variety of necklines can be cut for this blouse, such as square or round yokes. No measurements are given for the yokes as these need to be individually calculated.

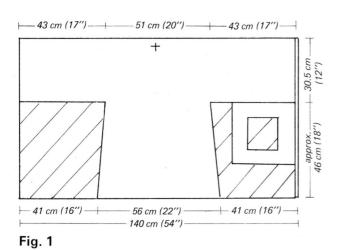

Fig. 1

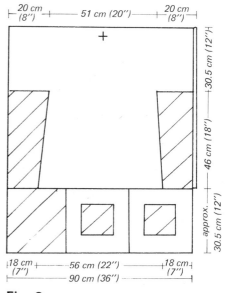

Fig. 2

104

the pieces. If using fabric with a one-way design or nap, cut fabric in half along fold. Turn one half so that fabric is the correct way up on back and front of garment. Place the two pieces right sides together and lay out fabric as shown in Figs 1 or 2.

If necessary, stitch 'shoulder' seams.

With right sides together, stitch the two yoke pieces round the inside edges of whatever shape has been chosen. Clip all curves or corners and turn right side out (Fig. 3). Turn in raw edges on both yoke pieces to wrong side and make sure that yoke lies flat.

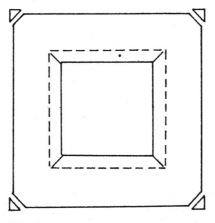

Fig. 3

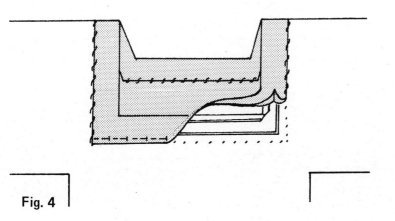

Fig. 4

Position yoke round neck opening and stitch to body on right and wrong sides of garment (Figs 4 and 5).

Stitch underarm and side seams (Fig. 6).

Hem the lower edges of sleeves and blouse. The sleeves can be left loose, or can be gathered up by inserting elastic into the sleeve hems.

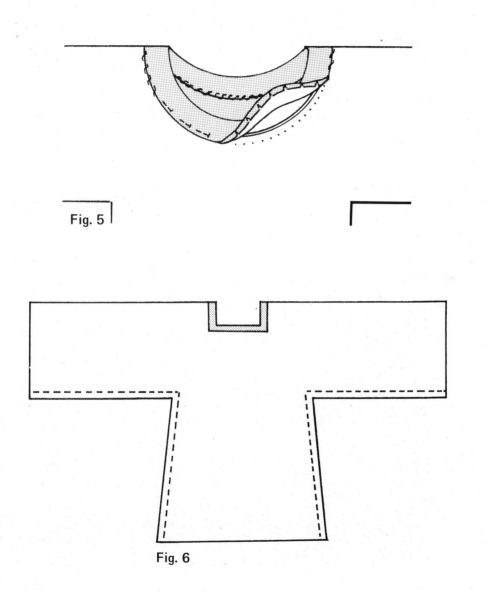

Fig. 5

Fig. 6

Four-piece dress or coat

Economy of fabric is achieved here by the interlocking construction of the garment. The fabric is folded in half and four identical pieces are cut out. The trapezium shape of the body makes the garment hang gracefully, even though the fit is a loose one. See the colour photograph facing page 64.

Fabric requirements

90 cm (36") fabric is required. Measure from shoulder to desired length, add 8 cm (3") for turnings plus another 30·5 cm (12"). Double the total of all these measurements, which will give you the length of fabric required. For example, a full-length dress would require approximately 3·7 m (4 yds) of 90 cm (36") fabric.

For a short, or knee-length, dress, the width of the base does not need to be as great as that needed for a full-length garment. Therefore, the pieces can be cut with less flare from the under arm to the hem.

Suitable fabrics include lightweight cottons, wools and blends. Avoid using fabrics with a one-way design or nap.

Making up

See page 30 for instructions on calculating necklines.

Fold fabric in half on the crosswise grain, with right sides together. Cut along fold. Lay out fabric as shown in Figs 1 or 2 and cut out the pieces. There will be four 30·5 cm (12") squares left over and these can be used for binding.

Stitch centre back seam. Stitch centre front seam, leaving 10 cm–15 cm (4"–6") open at neck (Fig. 3). The dress can then be easily pulled on over the head. For the coat, do not stitch centre front seam. Turn back centre front edges and hem.

Stitch 'overarm', underarm and side seams (Fig. 3).

Using bias strips made up from the extra fabric (see page 150), or purchased bias binding, finish the neckline, either by binding or facing. The binding, or facing, can be continued round front opening.

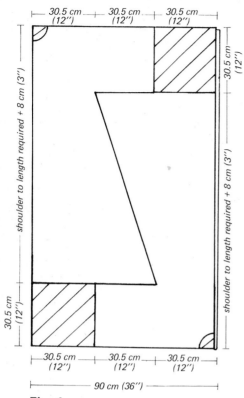

Fig. 1

30.5 cm (12") 30.5 cm (12") 30.5 cm (12")

shoulder to length required + 8 cm (3")

30.5 cm (12")

shoulder to length required + 8 cm (3")

30.5 cm (12")

30.5 cm (12") 30.5 cm (12") 30.5 cm (12")

90 cm (36")

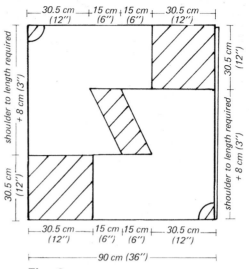

Fig. 2

30.5 cm (12") 15 cm (6") 15 cm (6") 30.5 cm (12")

shoulder to length required + 8 cm (3")

30.5 cm (12")

30.5 cm (12")

shoulder to length required + 8 cm (3")

30.5 cm (12") 15 cm (6") 15 cm (6") 30.5 cm (12")

90 cm (36")

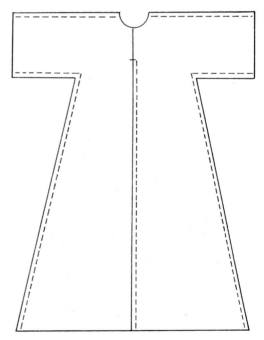

Fig. 3

Turn up and hem or bind lower edges of sleeves and body. If the sleeve edges or hemline dip at the sides, arc off the edges to ensure a smooth and even line (Fig. 4 and see page 33).

Attach a suitable fastening to front opening of dress or coat.

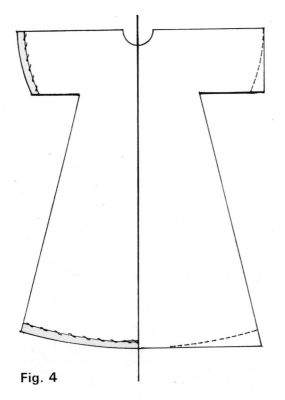

Fig. 4

Traditional caftans

Caftans have been worn for many years in the Mediterranean region, and in the Near and Middle East. It is a short or full-length, loose, shirt-type of garment and can be of a simple or complex cut. In the past, when material was scarce, garments were cut to economize on fabric as much as possible. Clothes were constructed from the least-worn parts of discarded garments, especially those parts that had been lavishly embroidered. The parts of a garment that received most wear would be renewed and patched again and again. This resulted in a garment of a more complex cut than was used in the original making up.

I have described an exceptionally simple type of caftan-like garment in the 'Four-piece dress or coat' on page 108. Here I have given instructions for two caftans of a more complex cut.

BRIDE'S CAFTAN

This type of caftan comes from the Holy Land and is traditionally worn by a bride. It is constructed from rectangles: one for the back and front of the body, two for the side gussets, two for the sleeves and one for the neck panel.

The material traditionally used for this caftan was natural-coloured linen, enriched with multi-coloured embroidery worked on the neck panel and main seams. An additional interesting feature is found at the lower back of the caftan, where a block, or panel, of embroidery is worked, extending to the sides.

Fabric requirements

For an average adult: 3 m ($3\frac{1}{4}$ yds) of 120 cm (48″) or 140 cm (54″) fabric. This is twice the desired length from shoulder to hem plus 10 cm (4″) for turnings. If using 90 cm (36″) fabric, you will need approximately 4 m ($4\frac{1}{3}$ yds). This is twice the desired length, plus 66 cm (26″) for sleeves, plus 33 cm (13″) for neck panel and 10 cm (4″) for turnings.

Scale down the layouts shown in Figs 1 and 2 for a child's size. Lengthen or shorten body and side gusset pieces for larger or smaller adult sizes. The most important measurement to remember is that from shoulder to hem.

All plain or non-directional patterned fabrics are suitable. Avoid using fabrics with a one-way design or nap.

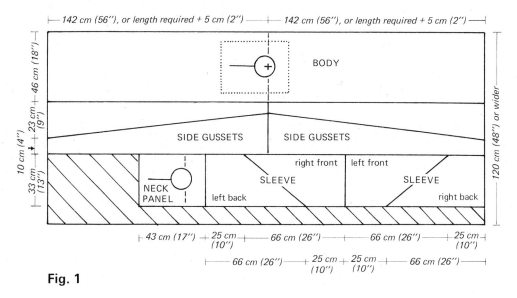

Fig. 1

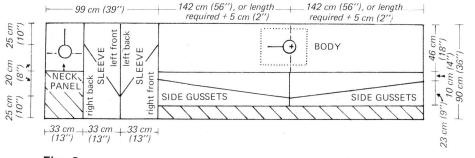

Fig. 2

Making up

See page 30 for instructions on calculating necklines.

Lay out fabric as shown in Figs 1 or 2 and cut out the pieces. Position neck panel over corresponding part of body piece and cut neck opening through both layers of fabric.

114

Stitch side gussets to front and back of body and at shoulders (Fig. 3).

Stitch 'overarm' seams of sleeves (Fig. 3).

Match the centre points of sides to centre points of sleeves and stitch sleeves to body piece (Fig. 4). Note that the garment is still in a flat form at this stage.

With right sides together, stitch underarm and side seams (Fig. 5).

Turn up and hem lower edges of sleeves and body.

The embroidery is worked after the caftan has been made up (Fig. 6). Traditionally, this is mostly worked in cross stitch. You can embroider the neck panel before it is attached to the body, or after it has been stitched in position.

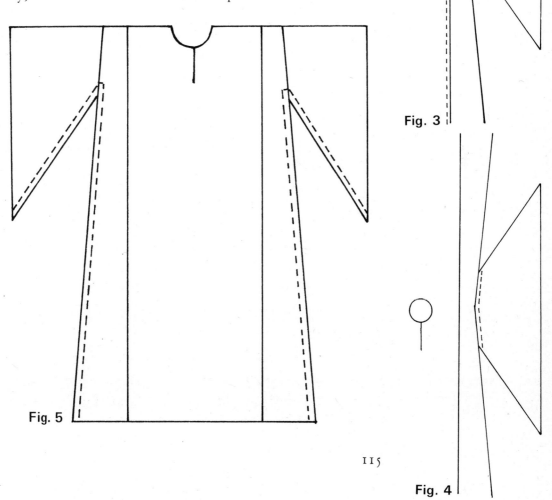

Fig. 3

Fig. 4

Fig. 5

Place the neck panel wrong side down on to right side of body piece. Turn in all raw edges and slipstitch to body. Bind neckline and front opening edges, or turn in neckline and front opening edges and slipstitch (Fig. 6).

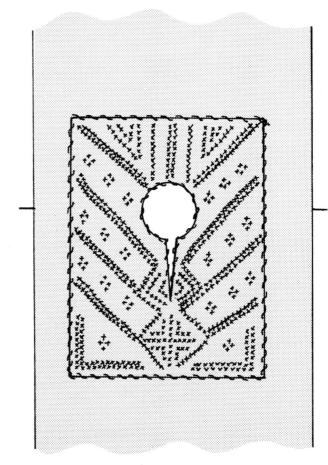

Fig. 6

MOROCCAN CAFTAN

The cut of a caftan varies throughout the regions in which it is worn. The Moroccan caftan described here is a clever construction of many pieces. The main differences between this caftan and the one from the Holy Land are the increased fullness and the rectangular sleeve form. The front has a longer opening and is fastened by loops and buttons. Traditionally, the sides of the garment are left open from beneath the gussets. Because of the fullness of this caftan, the side openings do not gape, but, of course, the sides can be stitched together.

Fabric requirements

For an average adult: 3·9 m (4¼ yds) of 90 cm (36″) fabric are required.

For larger sizes, use a wider width and increase the scale of the layout shown in Fig. 1.

Many types of fabrics are suitable for making up into a caftan, from the lightest cottons to heavy satins and brocades, lightweight woollens and woven or knitted blends. As such a lot of fabric is required, heavyweight wools or tweeds are not suitable as they would make the garment very heavy to wear. Avoid using fabrics with a one-way design or nap.

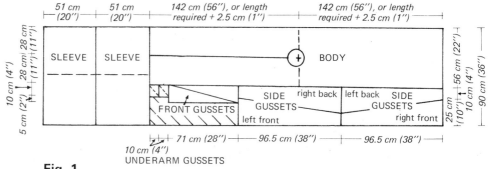

Fig. 1

Making up

See page 30 for instructions on calculating necklines.

Lay out fabric as shown in Fig. 1 and cut out the pieces. Stitch centre front gussets together, then position and stitch these to the centre front section of body (Fig. 2).

Pin side gussets to underarm section of each sleeve and stitch (Fig. 3). Match the centre points of sleeves to centre points of sides of body and stitch gussets and sleeves to body (Fig. 3). Note that the garment is still in a flat form at this stage.

Stitch underarm seams, leaving 5 cm (2″) open at the underarm ends of seams. Fold each underarm gusset in half diagonally. Pin and hand-stitch each gusset to right sides of underarm seams and side gussets (Fig. 4).

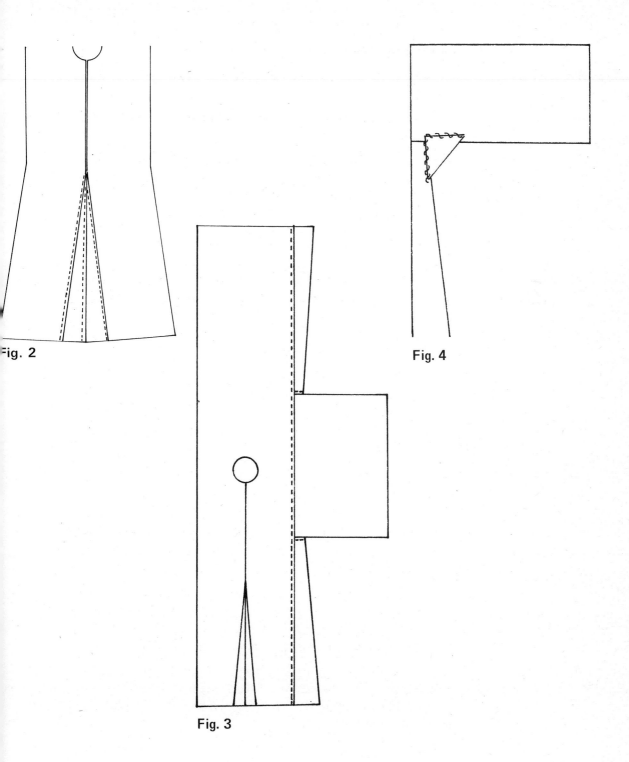

Fig. 2

Fig. 3

Fig. 4

Turn in and hem raw edges of side openings for an open-sided caftan, or stitch sides of garment together.

Finish neckline and front opening by binding with braid. Attach loops of braid for button fastenings and sew on buttons to correspond with the braid loops (Fig. 5).

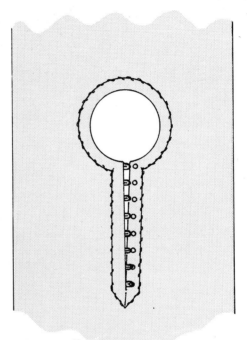

Fig. 5

Turn up and hem lower edges of sleeves and body.

Tubular skirts

There are numerous ways of wrapping a rectangular length of fabric round the waist and hips to form a skirt. In the Indonesian islands the rectangle is sewn into a tube and the skirt is formed by folding and pleating. There are different ways of tying the garment for men and women. The man's method requires little attention once the skirt is tied. The woman's method of tying, however, requires constant attention, but this is considered a feminine charm among the islanders. See the colour photograph facing page 65.

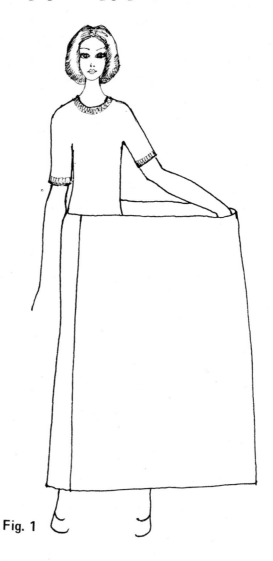

Fig. 1

Fabric requirements

For an average adult: approximately 1·8 m (2 yds) of 90 cm (36″) fabric. This is the length desired, plus 5 cm (2″) for turnings × the girth round your body, plus an arm's stretch away from the waist on one side (Fig. 1).

The fabrics that are most suitable are those that will hang in soft folds, thus preventing any bulkiness at the waist turnover. All patterned fabrics are suitable, but use the making-up method shown in Fig. 3 for fabrics with a one-way design or nap, or if a longer skirt is necessary. Batik- and tie-dyed fabrics are traditionally used, and the simple construction is ideal for precious hand-dyed fabrics.

Making up

The tube can be constructed in two ways. For non-directional patterned fabrics, fold rectangle in half and stitch the two raw edges together (Fig. 2). For fabrics with a one-way design or nap, or for a longer skirt, cut the rectangle in half and turn design correct way up on both pieces. Stitch the two sets of selvedges together and neaten the raw edges (Fig. 3).

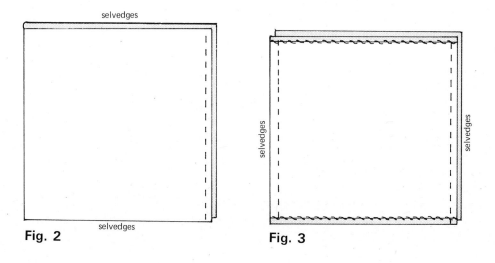

Fig. 2

Fig. 3

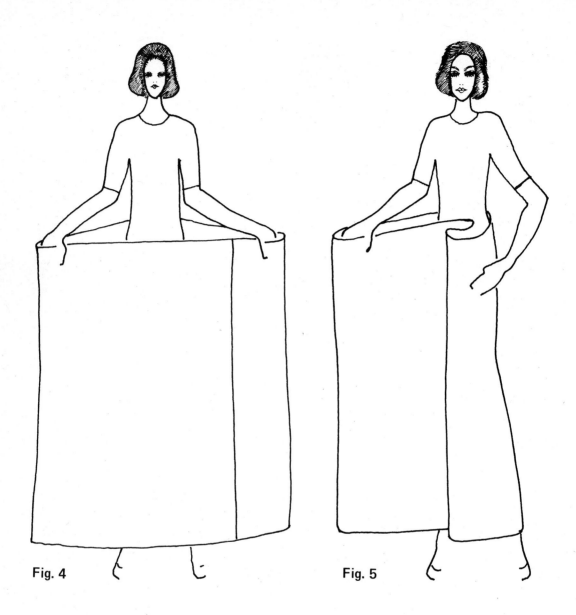

Fig. 4   Fig. 5

The skirt is now wrapped and tucked round the body. Hold out the tube at the sides (Fig. 4). Bring one side to the centre and make a pleat (Fig. 5). Bring the other side to the centre and make a second pleat, so that the skirt is tight round the waist (Fig. 6). It may be necessary to refold the first pleat to ensure a smooth fit. To keep pleats in place, roll over top of skirt twice (Fig. 7).

Fig. 6 Fig. 7 Fig. 8

The above is the man's method of folding and pleating the skirt and is the firmest one. The women tuck the end of the second pleat into the waist.

Another method of securing the tube is to hold it out to one side of the waist and make one pleat over the front of the body (Fig. 8). Tuck the end of this pleat into the waist. This leaves soft, diagonal folds across the skirt.

Triangular top

This top is made from a triangle, or from a square folded in half diagonally. It is tied at the neck and waist. See the colour photograph facing page 65.

Fabric requirements

For single thickness fabrics: 46 cm ($\frac{1}{2}$ yd) of 90 cm (36") fabric.
For double thickness fabrics: 61 cm ($\frac{2}{3}$ yd) of 90 cm (36") fabric.

All types of fabrics are suitable, from lightweight cottons to knitted jerseys. For very lightweight fabrics, use the square layout (Fig. 1) to give body to the top. For heavier fabrics, use the triangular layout (Fig. 2).

As a top made from the square layout is worn crossways, the pattern of a fabric should not be one-way. For example, if the fabric chosen has vertical stripes, when the top has been made up, these stripes will run across the top in a diagonal direction. This, of course, can look very attractive, but it may not be desirable with other patterned fabrics. If you are in any doubt, use the triangular layout shown in Fig. 2.

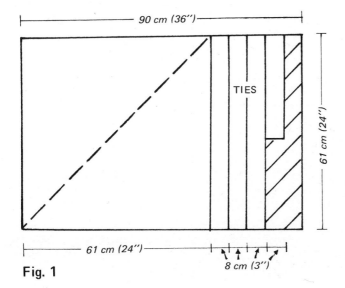

Fig. 1

Making up

Lay out fabric as shown in Figs 1 or 2 and cut out the pieces.

If using layout shown in Fig. 1, fold square in half diagonally, with right sides together. Stitch the sides, leaving 2·5 cm (1″) open at the two waist sides and a 13 cm (5″) opening at the neck (Fig. 3).

Turn right side out. Turn top flaps in 8 cm (3″) and oversew top edges together, leaving openings for the halter tie to be threaded through (Fig. 4). Turn in the two waist openings ready for the waist ties to be attached (Fig. 4).

If using layout shown in Fig. 2, turn in and hem the three sides of the triangle (Fig. 5).

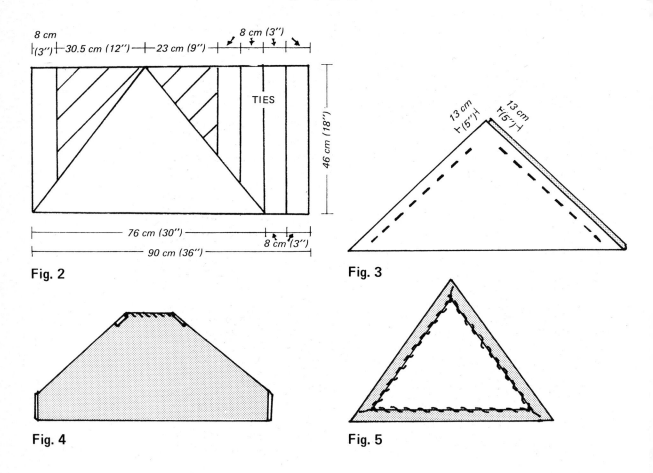

Fig. 2

Fig. 3

Fig. 4

Fig. 5

129

You will need two 61 cm (24") ties for the waist and one 92 cm (36") continuous tie for the neck. Fold each tie in half and, with right sides together, stitch 1 cm ($\frac{1}{2}$") from edge. Pull each tie through to the right side. Turn in raw edges at the ends and slipstitch. The ties can be cut from fabric on the straight grain or on the bias.

To attach ties to a top made from the square layout, slot the waist ties into the corresponding openings (Fig. 6). Stitch firmly in position. Thread neck tie through neck opening, but do not secure with stitching, as then the neckline can be slightly gathered if necessary (Fig. 6).

If you have made a top from the triangular layout, position waist ties to wrong side and stitch firmly in place (Fig. 7). Fold neck point of triangle 8 cm (3") over to wrong side. Stitch 2·5 cm (1") on either side of point of triangle (Fig. 7). Thread neck tie through this turnover.

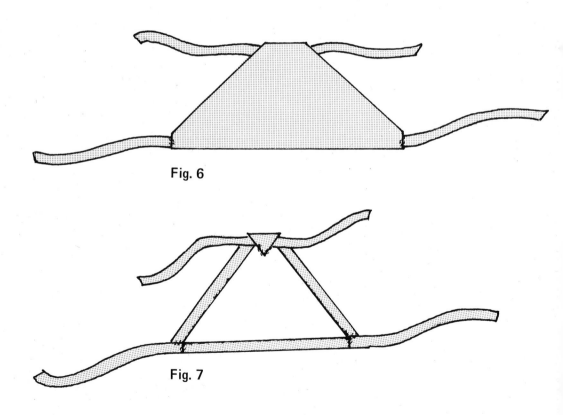

Fig. 6

Fig. 7

Wrap-around skirt

This garment is basically a semicircle with an arc for the waist and hem. Ties are attached to the waist, or to both waist and hip.

Fabric requirements

For a knee-length skirt: 1·8 m (2 yds) of 90 cm (36″) fabric.
For a full-length skirt: 2·4 m (2⅔ yds) of 120 cm (48″) fabric.
For larger or taller sizes, 2·7 m (3 yds) of 140 cm (54″) fabric are required.
For the waistband: allow an extra 12 cm–23 cm (⅛ yd–¼ yd) if using the same fabric. This is the waist arc of the skirt plus 61 cm (24″). If you want the band to be long enough to wrap completely round the waist, allow twice the waist arc of skirt plus 61 cm (24″). The width of the band should be 9 cm (3½″), to make a 2·5 cm (1″) wide band.

Most fabrics are suitable, but avoid choosing those with a one-way design or nap. If a striped fabric is used, it will slope horizontally across the back of the skirt and vertically down the front, which will create a pleasant rhythm round the skirt. Softer fabrics will drape more successfully for this type of garment.

Making up

Fold fabric in half crosswise with right sides together. The length of the waist arc should be your waist measurement plus enough for the wrapover, say, 5 cm (2″), and another 5 cm (2″) for turnings.

As the fabric is folded, the length of the arc line between points B and C is half the total length of the waist arc (Fig. 1).

To calculate AB (the radius of your waist circle), use the same formula as for the radius of a neckline (page 30). (Include the 10 cm (4″) for turnings and wrapover in your circumference calculations.)

For example, if your waist is 66 cm, add on the 10 cm, which equals 76 cm.

$$\frac{\text{circumference}}{\frac{22}{7}} = \text{diameter}$$

$$\frac{76 \times 7}{22} \text{ cancels down to } \frac{38 \times 7}{11} = \frac{266}{11} = 24 \text{ cm}$$

Therefore, the radius (line AB) is 12 cm.

The same calculation worked out in inches (waist = 26″, add on 4″ for turnings and wrapover, therefore, circumference = 30″):

$$\frac{30 \times 7}{22} \text{ cancels down to } \frac{15 \times 7}{11} = \frac{105}{11} = 9\tfrac{1}{2}''$$

Therefore, the radius (line AB) is $4\tfrac{3}{4}''$.

To mark the arc BC, pin a piece of string to point A. Attach a chalk pencil at required length and mark arc. This arc will be your stitching line. Mark another arc 2·5 cm (1″) inside first arc for cutting line.

Calculate length required for skirt and add on 5 cm (2″) for hem. Mark the bottom arc in the same way as the waist arc (Fig. 1).

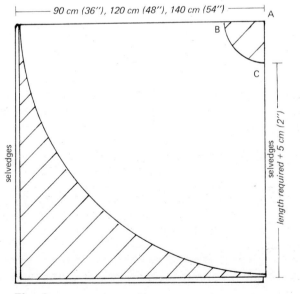

Fig. 1

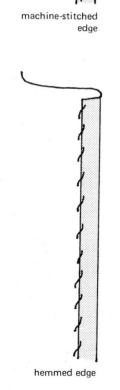

machine-stitched
edge

hemmed edge

Fig. 2

Neaten the two straight edges of skirt by turning 2·5 cm (1″) to the wrong side and hemming or machine-stitching (Fig. 2). As these are selvedges, they are only turned under once.

The waist needs a firm binding that can be extended to be the ties of the skirt. This can be made from contrasting fabric, or ribbon, or can be cut from the same fabric as the skirt.

Centre the band along the right side of the waist arc, with the ties extending at both ends. Stitch firmly to waist 2·5 cm (1″) from edge (Fig. 3). Turn band over to wrong side, turn under raw edge 1 cm ($\frac{1}{2}$″) and hem to skirt (Fig. 4). To make the diagrams clearer, Figs 3 and 4 do not show the ties.

Turn in raw edges and ends of rest of band and slipstitch these edges together.

Turn up hem to required length and stitch (Fig. 5).

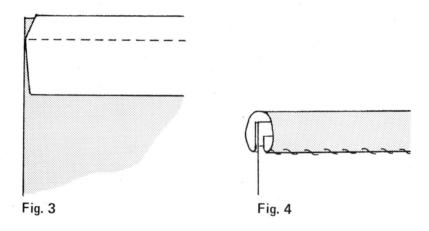

Fig. 3   **Fig. 4**

Additional ties can be attached at hip level, if the skirt tends to gape. Make up two 2·5 cm (1″) wide ties as for waist ties. Mark position of ties on skirt and stitch ties in place.

There are many alternatives to the instructions given above. For example, if contrasting fabric is used for the waistband and ties, this could be continued as a decorative trim down the length of the skirt and round the hem. To calculate the extra amount of fabric required for this, measure the two overlap lengths of the skirt and the circumference of the hem. Attach binding as for waist.

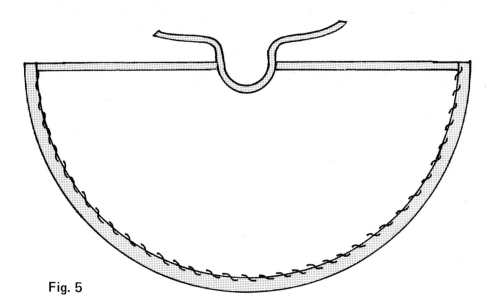

Fig. 5

If you wish to have a concealed waist binding, a firm 2·5 cm (1″) wide tape is required, and should be 2·5 cm (1″) longer than the waist arc. Stitch tape to right side of waist arc, 1 cm ($\frac{1}{2}$″) from edge (Fig. 6). Turn tape to wrong side. Turn in the ends and hem firmly to skirt (Fig. 7). The waist and hip can be fastened by attaching hooks and bars.

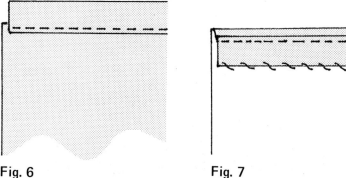

Fig. 6   **Fig. 7**

For a skirt without a wrapover, the two straight sides can be stitched together, leaving 15 cm–20 cm (6″–8″) open at waist. The 5 cm (2″) used for the wrapover will prevent the skirt from gaping. The skirt can be fastened by hooks and bars, or ties. This type of skirt will not fit as tightly on the hips as the wrap-around skirt.

Semicircular cloak

This full flowing cloak is made from one piece of fabric, a semicircle, with an arc cut at the neck and shoulder slits cut and overlapped for a good fit on the shoulders. As an optional extra, a two-piece hood can be cut from the spare fabric. See the colour photograph facing page 49.

Fabric requirements

The length of the cloak depends on the wearer's height and the width of fabric used. To calculate length of fabric required, allow 15 cm (6") for neck arc, then measure from neck to length required. Add on another 5 cm (2") for a hem, if necessary. Double this length for fabric required, bearing in mind that the total length of the cloak must fit within the width of fabric being used.

For a small child: 1·8 m (2 yds) of 90 cm (36") fabric will make a full-length cloak.
For a small adult: 1·8 m (2 yds) of 90 cm (36") fabric will make a knee- or hip-length cloak. 2·7 m (3 yds) of 120 cm (48") or 140 cm (54") fabric will make a full-length cloak.
For an average adult: 2·7 m (3 yds) of 120 cm (48") or 140 cm (54") fabric will make a knee-length cloak. 3·3 m (3½ yds) of 150 cm (60") fabric will make a mid-calf to full-length cloak.

Suitable fabrics to choose are all types of warm woven fabrics in plain or all-over patterns, regular checks or stripes. Reversible fabrics are ideal as the cloak can be worn either side out. Avoid using fabrics with a one-way design or nap, and avoid knitted fabrics because of their tendency to stretch out of shape when used for full-length garments.

Making up

Lay out fabric as shown in Fig. 1. Chalk or pin a 15 cm (6") arc for the neck from the centre point of one long side. Or calculate radius of neck as described on page 30. The neck and hood measurements given in Fig. 1 are for an average adult.

To calculate neckline for other sizes of cloak:

1 Measure base of neck.
2 Add 8 cm (3") for ease.
3 Add 5 cm–8 cm (2"–3") for darts, depending on slope of shoulders.
4 Add 5 cm (2") for front turnings.
5 If necessary, add on another 5 cm (2") for overlap at front of cloak.

The total of Nos 1–5 = measurement of semicircular stitching line of neck.

Calculate length required, add on 5 cm (2") for turnings, if necessary, and chalk or pin another arc for the bottom of the cloak, using the same centre point as that used for the neck arc. Cut out fabric on these two arcs.

Fold fabric in half, making two quarter circles out of the neck arc. Mark the centre point of each quarter arc and cut two shoulder slits 15 cm–18 cm (6"–7") long (Fig. 1).

A hood can be cut from two rectangles using the leftover fabric (Fig. 1).

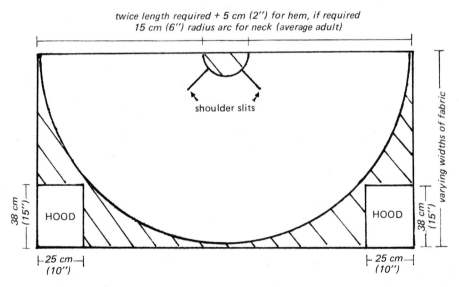

Fig. 1

138

With right sides together, stitch shoulder slits into darts, measuring 2·5 cm–4 cm ($1''$–$1\frac{1}{2}''$) at neck edge and tapering to a point 1 cm ($\frac{1}{2}''$) beyond the end of slit (Fig. 2). Trim darts to 1 cm ($\frac{1}{2}''$) and neaten edges by hemming to fabric (Fig. 3).

If a hood is to be attached, stitch two sides of the rectangles with right sides together (Fig. 4). With right sides together, pin hood to neck, matching front edges, and stitch in place, clipping where necessary (Fig. 4).

All raw edges should be firmly hemmed or bound. If a reversible fabric is used, bind all edges and stitch a strip of binding over each dart to cover raw edges.

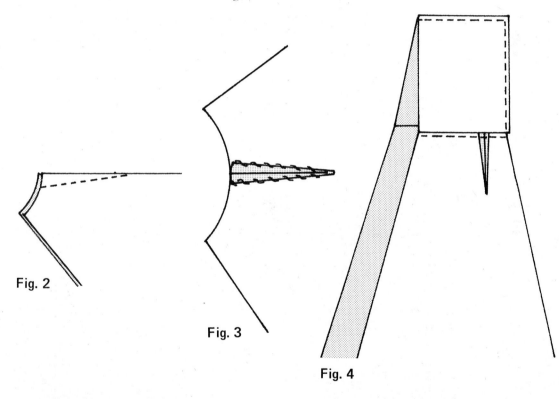

Fig. 2

Fig. 3

Fig. 4

Fasten cloak by attaching ties, buttons and loops, or by stitching decorative frogged fastenings at the neck and at 15 cm ($6''$) intervals down front of cloak. When using reversible fabrics, make sure that fastenings can be reached when wearing the cloak either side out.

Full-length cloak for adults

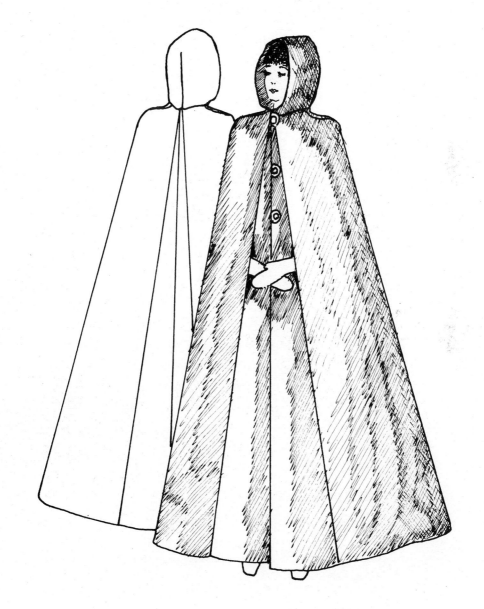

This cloak is not as full at the base as the 'Semicircular cloak', but it makes an economical use of the fabric.

Fabric requirements

To calculate the length of fabric required, measure from neck over shoulder to required length, plus 5 cm (2″) for turnings, if necessary. Double this measurement.

For an average adult: 3 m (3⅓ yds) of 140 cm (54″) fabric. Add on an extra 30·5 cm (⅓ yd) for a hood.

The layout shown in Fig. 1 can be easily adjusted for taller or shorter adults.

Most fabrics are suitable, from warm wools, worsteds and wool blends, to lightweight wind- and showerproof fabrics, such as ciré. A brocade-type fabric would make an attractive evening cloak. Avoid using stretchy knitted fabrics, or those with a one-way design or nap.

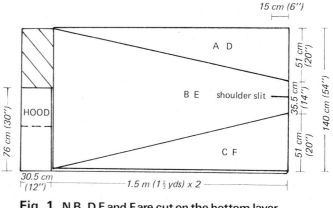

Fig. 1 N.B. D, E and F are cut on the bottom layer of fabric.

Making up

Lay out fabric as shown in Fig. 1. The fabric is folded, right sides together, and cut along the fold for pieces A, B, C, D, E and F, but the hood is cut from a single layer of fabric. Cut out the pieces and label them to avoid confusion. Mark centres of pieces B and E for shoulder slits.

142

Position and pin pieces together: C to B to A to F to E to D (Fig. 2). Slits can be left for arms between panels C and B, and D and E. These slits should be 15 cm (6″) long and should start 38 cm (15″) from neck edge. Stitch panels together (Fig. 2). Turn raw edges of arm slits to wrong side and stitch.

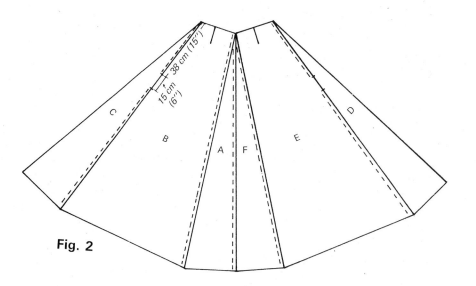

Fig. 2

×

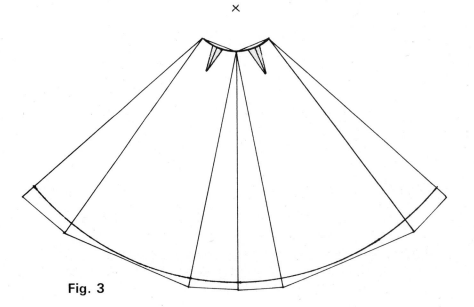

Fig. 3

Trim neckline to form a shallow curve (Fig. 3). Arc off bottom edge by finding the point where the radiating lines meet beyond the neck of cloak and mark arc as for semi-circular cloak (Fig. 3 and see pages 33–35).

Cut the two shoulder slits 15 cm–18 cm (6″–7″) long and make darts as for semicircular cloak (Fig. 3 and see page 139).

Attach hood to cloak and finish raw edges and darts as for semicircular cloak. Or finish panels with run and fell seams (see page 147). Where a reversible fabric has been used, it will be necessary to bind all panel seams, thus making a decorative feature of the panels. Attach a suitable fastening to front opening.

Basic hand-sewing techniques

Traditionally, all garments were hand-sewn before the sewing machine was invented. Listed here are some simple stitching and finishing techniques for hand-sewing.

Seams

Most hand-stitched seams are worked from right to left, placing the garment towards you and the edge of the seam away from you.

A plain seam is formed by small, even running stitches (Fig. 1). The smaller the stitches, the more secure the seam.

A back-stitched seam is used when greater strength is required (Fig. 2).

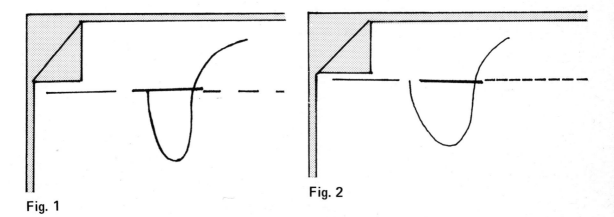

Fig. 1

Fig. 2

When the seams are stitched they are pressed open (Fig. 3), or over to one side (Fig. 4).

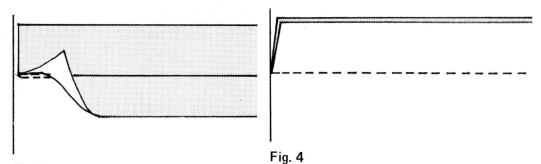

Fig. 3

Fig. 4

The seams are then neatened to prevent the fabric fraying and this can be done in a variety of ways, of which only three are given here. Some fabrics, such as jersey or felt, need no neatening, but most fabrics will fray with wear and laundering.

Overcasting is the simplest method of neatening a seam. The needle and thread pass through the seam edge only (Fig. 5). The stitches should be slanted and worked approximately 3 mm ($\frac{1}{8}$″) deep and 6 mm ($\frac{1}{4}$″) apart. Do not pull up the thread too tightly or the fabric will pucker.

Blanket stitch gives a firm and neat edge to seams that are liable to fray. Work from left to right with stitches 3 mm ($\frac{1}{8}$″) deep and apart, or work larger stitches, depending on the bulkiness of the fabric. Put needle in straight through edge and make a loop by holding the thread under the point of the

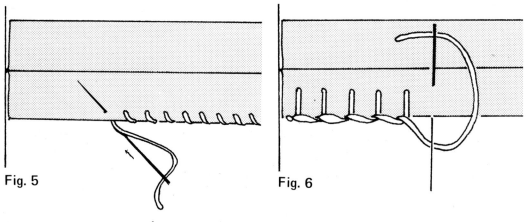

Fig. 5

Fig. 6

needle. Pull needle through loop and proceed to next stitch (Fig. 6). This stitch can also be used as a decorative finish on garments such as the ponchos.

A herringbone-finished seam is worked from left to right. Insert the needle, from right to left, in seam edge, but only pick up a few threads of the fabric. Make a corresponding stitch in the garment fabric (Fig. 7). This stitch is used on heavyweight fabrics for a seam that is not bulky and that lies flat, and on fabrics that fray badly. It is also used as a hemming stitch and is sometimes referred to as catch-stitch.

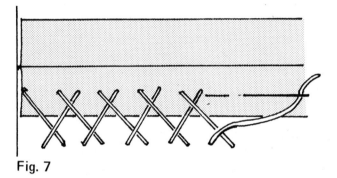

Fig. 7

A more complex seam, but one which was traditionally used because of its strength, is called run and fell (also known as flat fell). In this book, garments such as the shirt and the smocks, would originally have all been sewn by this method of seaming. This seam would also work well in stitching the panels of the full-length cloak and other reversible garments.

Place edges to be stitched right sides together (Fig. 8). Stitch and trim one edge to 1 cm ($\frac{1}{2}''$) and the other edge to 6 mm ($\frac{1}{4}''$).

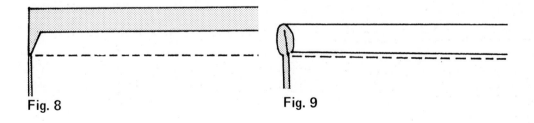

Fig. 8   Fig. 9

Fold the 1 cm (½″) turning over the 6 mm (¼″) turning. Then fold both turnings flat on to garment (Fig. 9). Pin or tack in position and hem down (Fig. 10). When using hemming stitch, pick up only one or two threads of the garment fabric, so that stitches show as little as possible.

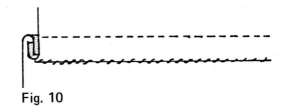

Fig. 10

An oversewn seam is used to join two selvedges or already hemmed edges, and is worked from right to left. The stitches should be as small and as close together as possible (Fig. 11). This seam is used when joining the serape edges together. An oversewn seam is referred to as 'whipping' when joining lace to an edge.

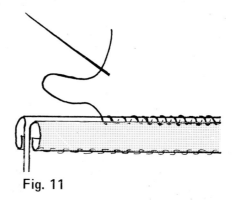

Fig. 11

A french seam is a very strong seam that neatens itself. Only use this seam on thin fabrics as otherwise it can become bulky, but it is very useful in seaming sheer fabrics as it neatly hides the stitching.

With wrong sides together, pin fabric on fitting lines. Stitch a plain or back-stitched seam 6 mm (¼″) inside the fitting line (Fig. 12). Trim surplus of seam to 3 mm (⅛″) and remove pins.

Turn work right sides together and fold over on the seam line. Pin or tack on fitting lines and stitch along these, enclosing the raw edges (Fig. 13).

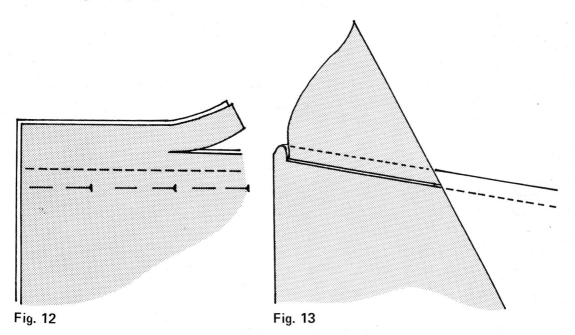

Fig. 12   **Fig. 13**

Bias binding and bias facing

Throughout the book a finish that is widely used is called bias binding, sometimes called crossway binding. Because of its stretchy quality, it can act as a narrow facing to a garment, instead of having to cut a shaped facing.

A bias binding means that the binding can be seen on both wrong and right sides of the garment. A bias facing is only seen on the wrong side of the garment.

Bias binding (or straight binding) can be bought in many different colours, or can be cut from the same fabric as the garment. Some of the garments in this book have enough wastage that can be used for cutting out bias, or straight, strips.

149

To make your own bias strips, you must first find the true bias, or direct cross, of the fabric. In order to do this, you must also know something about the construction of a woven fabric. Fig. 14 shows the grain and bias of a one-way fabric.

The selvedge is the firmer, woven lengthwise edge on either side of a width of fabric. The warp threads are the lengthwise threads of the fabric. The weft threads are the threads that weave across the width of the fabric.

Fold over the crosswise edge to the selvedge, or lengthwise edge, of the fabric, to form a right-angled triangle. The true bias is the line between the 45° angles (Figs 14 and 15).

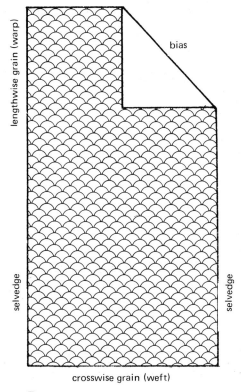

Fig. 14

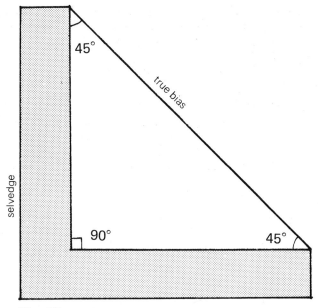

Fig. 15

A bias strip can be cut to any width, but 2·5 cm (1″) is the usual size. Mark off parallel strips, 2·5 cm (1″) wide, with pins or chalk. The longer the strips, the less joins you will need to make. Note that the 2·5 cm (1″) should be measured at right angles to the true bias. Cut strips on marked lines (Fig. 16).

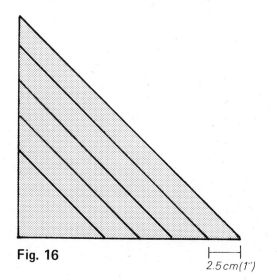

Fig. 16

2.5 cm (1″)

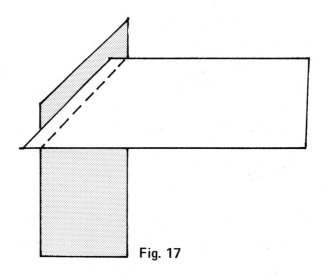

Fig. 17

To join bias strips, place right sides together at an angle of 45°
and allow the edges to cross over 6 mm ($\frac{1}{4}$") for turnings (Fig.
17). Stitch and press open (Fig. 18). Trim extending points.

To attach bias binding as a decorative trim, cut the bias strip
four times the finished width of trim. For example, the trim
will be 6 mm ($\frac{1}{4}$") wide if bias is cut 2·5 cm (1") wide.

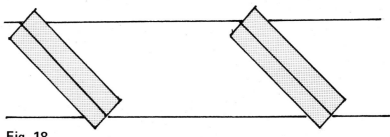

Fig. 18

Place right side of strip to right side of garment with the top
edge of strip below edge of garment (Fig. 19). Stretch the strip
round concave curves and ease it over convex curves (Fig. 19).

Tack and stitch a quarter of the width of the strip to the
fitting, or stitching, line (Fig. 19). Trim seam allowance down
to edge of bias strip (Fig. 20).

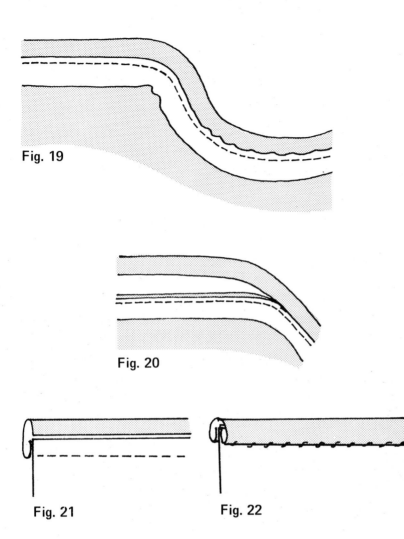

Fig. 19

Fig. 20

Fig. 21   Fig. 22

Press bias strip up and fold it over to wrong side. Turn in raw edge of strip to meet other edges (Fig. 21).

Hem folded edge of bias strip to first stitching line (Fig. 22).

When stitching bias binding round an inside corner, pin or tack binding to stitching line, pulling it tight round the corner. This will form a pleat in the bias binding at the corner. When hemming the binding to the wrong side, make a small inverted pleat so that the binding tucks neatly into the corner (Fig. 23). Slipstitch the pleat to hold it in place.

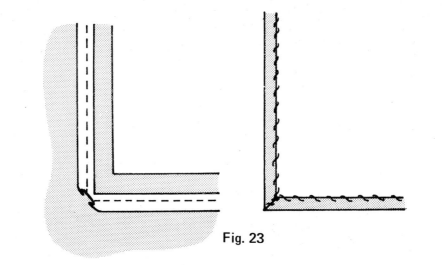

Fig. 23

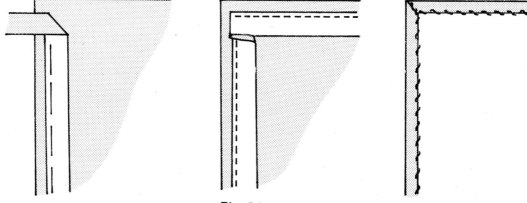

Fig. 24

To attach bias binding to outside corners, pin or tack binding on the stitching line up to the corner on one side. Turn binding at right angles to the first edge and form a diagonal fold at the corner (Fig. 24). Turn folded binding back on itself, forming a pleat. Pin or tack binding along second side of corner. Do not stitch through the pleat, but take the stitching up to the pleat on the first side of the corner and start stitching again just beyond the pleat along the second side of the corner. When hemming the binding to the wrong side, make an inverted pleat in the binding at the corner (Fig. 24). Slipstitch the pleat to hold it in place.

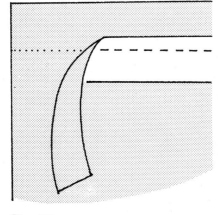

Fig. 25

To attach a bias strip as a facing, cut the bias strips twice as wide as the finished width of facing. For example, the facing will be 1 cm ($\frac{1}{2}''$) wide if the strip is cut 2·5 cm (1") wide. Place right side of strip to right side of garment with the strip a quarter of its width over the stitching line (Fig. 25). Ease strip round concave curves and stretch round convex curves. This is because when the facing is turned to the wrong side, the stitched concave curve will become a convex curve, and vice versa.

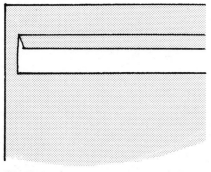

Fig. 26

Tack and stitch bias strip to stitching line (Fig. 25). Press down turning of strip only, as this will make the seam come just over the wrong side of the garment when the strip is turned over (Fig. 26). Trim seam allowance of garment to 6 mm ($\frac{1}{4}''$).

155

Turn bias strip completely to wrong side and turn in raw edge of strip to meet other edges (Fig. 27). Hem down folded edge of strip to garment (Fig. 27).

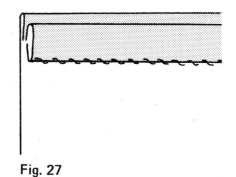

Fig. 27

When attaching a concealed bias strip to corners, tack the strip to the garment on the stitching line, making pleats in strip at inner and outer corners as in bias binding (Fig. 28). Turn in raw edge of strip and press (Fig. 28).

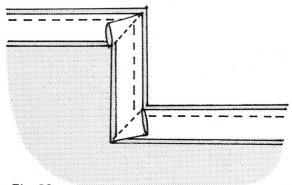

Fig. 28

Stitch the pleats at all corners to make bias strip lie flat (Fig. 28). Trim pleats and press open (Fig. 29). Turn strip completely to wrong side and hem folded edge of strip to garment.

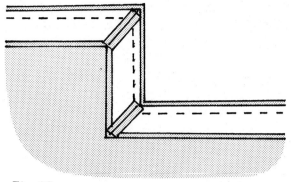

Fig. 29

Bias binding and facing are used more frequently than straight binding or tape. As they are cut on the cross they have a degree of elasticity that a straight binding does not have. Straight bindings, or tape, have more strength, but are only used on straight edges, or to stop a curved edge from stretching, e.g. the waist of the wrap-around skirt.

Rouleau strips

Rouleau means round or rolled. Throughout this book rouleau is mentioned as a decorative trim, or for use as button loops or ties. It is not necessary, therefore, to make up long lengths of rouleau as this is difficult to turn right side out.

Rouleau strips are made from bias strips of fabric. Fold bias strip in half along its length, with right side inside. Stitch these two layers together, one-third of the distance from the edges (Fig. 30).

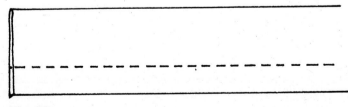

Fig. 30

157

To turn strip right side out, fasten a bodkin or safety pin at one end of strip. Push the bodkin or pin through the middle of strip, easing the outer side of strip inwards and the bodkin or pin up through the strip (Fig. 31).

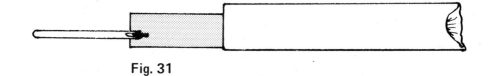

Fig. 31

Press rouleau strip with seamed edges on one side (Fig. 32).

Fig. 32

Further reading

The following books will provide further information on subjects allied to clothes construction that are not covered in this book. The selection is necessarily limited and only represents a small part of the many relevant books available.

Armes, Alice: *English Smocks* (Dryad Press)
Butler, Ann: *Simple Stitches* (Batsford)
Clucas, Joy: *Your Machine for Embroidery* (Bell)
Dyer, Anne and Duthoit, Valerie: *Canvas Work from the Start* (Bell)
Goldsworthy, Maureen: *Knowing Your Sewing* (Mills & Boon)
Green, Sylvia: *Patchwork for Beginners* (Studio Vista)
Harvey, Virginia, I.: *Colour and Design in Macramé* (Van Nostrand Reinhold)
Howard, Constance: *Inspiration for Embroidery* (Batsford)
Jameson, Norma: *Batik for Beginners* (Studio Vista)
Ladbury, Ann: *The Batsford Book of Sewing* (Batsford)
Maile, Anne: *Tie & Dye Made Easy* (Mills & Boon)
Risley, Christine: *Creative Embroidery; Machine Embroidery* (Studio Vista)
Robinson, Stuart: *Exploring Fabric Printing* (Mills & Boon)
Short, Eirian: *Introducing Macramé* (Batsford)
Thomas, Mary: *Book of Knitting Patterns; Dictionary of Embroidery Stitches* (Hodder & Stoughton)
Waller, Irene: *Designing with Thread, From Fibre to Fabric* (Studio Vista)
Whyte, Kathleen: *Design in Embroidery* (Batsford)
Williams, Elsa, S.: *Bargello Florentine Canvas Work* (Van Nostrand Reinhold).

Some of these titles may be out of print but could still be available at your local library.

Useful addresses

The number of craftsmen and craftswomen working in this country and abroad is endless. Therefore, the addresses of the following organizations are given rather than individually listing people who are involved with any one craft. By writing to the relevant address below, you can obtain information on the craft in which you are particularly interested.

Crafts Advisory Committee
12 Waterloo Place
London SW1Y 4AU
England

American Crafts Council
44 West 53rd Street
New York
N.Y. 10019
U.S.A.

Crafts Council of Australia
113 George Street
Sydney
N.S.W. 2000
Australia